Comprehension *Through* Conversation

The Power of Purposeful Talk in the Reading Workshop

M A R I A   N I C H O L S

HEINEMANN
Portsmouth, NH

KH

Heinemann

361 Hanover Street
Portsmouth, NH 03801–3912
www.heinemann.com

Offices and agents throughout the world

The author and publisher wish to thank those who have generously given permission to reprint borrowed material:

Table 2.1 adapted from *First Steps Oral Language Developmental Continuum*. Copyright © 1994 by Education Department of Western Australia. Used with permission from Harcourt Education, a division of Reed International Books Australia Pty Ltd.

Library of Congress Cataloging-in-Publication Data
Nichols, Maria.
   Comprehension through conversation : the power of purposeful talk in the reading workshop / Maria Nichols ; foreword by Richard L. Allington.
       p.   cm.
   Includes bibliographical references and index.
   ISBN-13: 978-0-325-00793-9
   ISBN-10: 0-325-00793-4 (pbk. : alk. paper)
   1. Reading comprehension—Study and teaching (Elementary).   2. Language arts (Elementary).   3. Conversation—Study and teaching (Elementary).   I. Title.

LB1573.7.N53 2006
372.47—dc22   2006014778

Acquisitions editor: Lois Bridges
Editor: Gloria Pipkin
Production service: Matrix Productions Inc.
Production coordinator: Lynne Costa
Cover design: Night & Day Design
Cover photograph: Maria Nichols
Typesetter: Kim Arney
Manufacturing: Steve Bernier

Printed in the United States of America on acid-free paper
10 09   RRD   4 5

10/13/09

Contents

For Rick, who encourages
with curiosity and understanding.

Foreword

One has to wonder about the early promise of standards-based reforms—that they would bring us vibrant classrooms, rich with a focus on understanding the world and how it was changing. I say "wonder" because in far too many classrooms today there is a tight focus on *remembering,* not a focus on *understanding.* Too often today, tightly scripted lessons move kids through a commercial curriculum largely devoid of any emphasis on helping children understand anything.

These are not the classrooms that Maria Nichols describes in this slender but powerful book. Instead, she describes classrooms where rich conversations replace mindless interrogations, where kids pursue the "I wonder" and "why," not just the "who," "what," "where," and "when."

The lessons in these classrooms reflect the sorts of lessons that Peter Johnston and I (2002) wrote about in our book describing the learning environments we observed in some of the nation's very best classrooms. But Nichols goes a step further than we did by setting out the nature of the conversations with several examples of lessons that portray the conversations these very lucky children experience day after day.

She presents us with the conversational dialogues occurring in these classrooms and then helps us see how children acquire deep understandings of texts and topics. Her rich examples suggest that this sort of instruction need not be limited to a few classrooms, but rather is attainable for each one.

Nichols offers not possible lessons, but full descriptions of actual lessons. Here you'll find no ivory-tower examples of what might be, but examples of what is already available in many classrooms. These are classrooms of the sort that we hope our children and grandchildren are lucky enough to encounter—not once in a while, but routinely. These are classrooms that are still uncommon, but the sort of classrooms that I hope will soon be the standard in schools.

As you read this book it will become obvious, I think, that remembering what was read is a poor substitute for *understanding* what was read. You will understand why one young learner, Troy, says during a reading conference, "I'm reading slow because of all the talking in my head!"

There is a lot more to proficient reading, a lot more to thoughtful literacy, than recording the speed at which children read aloud. A lot more. Reading *Comprehension Through Conversation* will drive that point home.

Reference: Allington, Richard, and Peter Johnston. 2002. *Reading to Learn: Lessons from Exemplary Fourth-Grade Classrooms*. New York: Guilford.

Richard L. Allington
University of Tennessee

Acknowledgments

None of us is as smart as all of us.
—Ken Blanchard

My journey into the exploration of purposeful talk began many years ago in a staff meeting. As the term "accountable talk" was being introduced, I distinctly remember leaning over to a colleague and whispering, "My kids talk. What's the big deal?" This discrepancy between the importance of talk in my mind and the importance others seemed to be placing on it stuck with me, and a classroom-based inquiry was born!

Years later, on a breathless Day One of a weeklong Reading and Writing Institute in San Diego, Richard Allington delighted the audience with a keynote focused on his research with Peter Johnston of exemplary teachers. Allington outlined a list of what he and Johnston termed the six T's, or common features, of exemplary teaching. Talk was high on the list. Allington's assertion that conversational talk was still underresearched was the impetus I needed to begin broadening my own focus on talk.

My exploration of talk, as with all my professional learning, has not been a solo journey. As I reflect on the friends and colleagues I've been privileged to think, talk, and learn beside, I'm reminded of an Oscar-weekend radio interview of composer and conductor Bill Conti. Conti was chatting with National Public Radio's *Wait, Wait, Don't Tell Me!* hosts about conducting for the Oscars. He joked about being connected by earphone to the production crew, who would prompt him to "cue up the music" when an award recipient droned on too long. I actually watched a bit of the Oscars that Sunday night, for no other reason than to listen for the orchestra to serenade long-winded stars offstage. I do admit to enjoying it!

However, I now feel more sympathy for those who received the musical "hook." How does one thank all those who have journeyed alongside us without a Bill Conti cueing the orchestra? I'll try.

I carried my inquiry and developing understanding of talk with me as I took on the role of Literacy Demonstration Teacher in the newly developed Literacy Professional Development Center for San Diego City Schools. The Professional Development Center was designed to explore and build conversations around cutting-edge pedagogical practices. For three years, alongside my friends and colleagues Peg Crane and Lynda Elliott, I divided my time between literacy instruction with a class of children, a core of which looped with me from first grade through to third grade, and the exploration of content and instructional practices with the extraordinary teachers, staff developers, and administrators of the San Diego City Schools.

My thank-you's begin with Peg, Lynda, and the children from the Professional Development Center classroom. Peg and Lynda brought incredible knowledge, experience, and joy to our work. And, without a doubt, the children were the most amazing group I have ever been privileged to learn alongside. Their thinking and voices are not only woven into this text, but are the driving force behind my commitment to the value of talk as a constructivist mechanism. I have seen firsthand what children can do when taught to think and to use talk purposefully as a tool for constructing knowledge.

I am appreciative of former San Diego City Schools Superintendent Alan Bersin's resolve in bringing a focus on professional development to San Diego. Under his leadership, voices from across the United States and around the world joined us in constructive conversations about teaching and learning. I am indebted to consultants Debra Crouch, Virginia Lockwood Zisa, Lyn Reggett, and Kaye Lawson for adding their voices to these conversations, and their wisdom. The Literacy Department, led by Director Staci Monreal and Assistant Director Jennifer White, became the center for these conversations, and I am stronger in my practice as a result. I thank Staci and Jennifer for their vision.

My new role as Literacy Staff Developer at Webster Academy of Science and Research, a low socioeconomic urban elementary school in the San Diego Unified School District, has allowed my research on talk in a constructivist environment to flourish. Once a low-performing school, Webster has made remarkable gains due to an extraordinary staff of dedicated professionals. In her new role as administrator at Webster Elementary, Jennifer White encourages teachers to focus on student engagement and the creation of a place where learning is both respected and celebrated. Jennifer's eyes shine when she speaks of classrooms where children "slurp up learning." Along with Jennifer, I am privileged to work closely with literacy support staff Teri Coker and Alexis Conerty, vice principal Marisol Marin, and math resource teacher Lisa Ann deGarcia, as well as an amazing group of teachers who have taken on the challenge of enabling Webster's wonderfully vibrant children to use talk as a tool for negotiating meaning. You will meet teachers Susie Althof, Jesse Harrison, Stephanie Hasselbrink, Marika Nieratko, Jeralyn Treas, and Stacie Wright in the pages of this book.

Prior to Webster Elementary, I had the opportunity to practice alongside Chas Moriarty, administrator of Garfield Elementary, as he worked tirelessly to transform this traditionally low-performing urban elementary school into an orchestration of lively classrooms where children talk purposefully. In Chapter 4, you will meet Garfield first-grade teacher Maricela Cruz, who took to heart the importance of creating an environment where children think and talk purposefully together.

I am stronger in my practice thanks to conversations with longtime friends and colleagues who value struggling with tough questions about teaching and learning as much as I do. I thank Brenda Allen, Bill and Pat Eastman, Cherisa Kreider, Sylvia McGrade, Catherine Bogart Martinez, Cindy Marten, and Lisa Miller for their professional passion and camaraderie.

For many summers, I traveled to New York City to attend the Teacher's College Reading and Writing Project at Columbia University. Led by Lucy Calkins, Laurie Pessah, and a talented team of staff developers, these institutes were a yearly intellectual sojourn that allowed me to immerse myself in rigorous learning and reflect on my own practice. My belief in the importance of talk grew as the Teacher's College staff shared their yearlong conversations, for which I thank them.

For writers, taking pencil to paper has all but been replaced by fingers that dance over keyboards. Sometimes they dance deftly; at other times, they push wrong keys and make huge technical messes. I am indebted to my neighbor and friend, Dave Roger, for getting me out of more of these messes as I wrote than I care to admit to. He truly holds a seat of honor among "computer geeks"!

And of course, where would a writer be without the wisdom of her editor? I was blessed with the guidance of two extraordinary editors, Gloria Pippin and Lois Bridges. It is their mindfulness around focus and purpose, along with support from Lynne Costa, production editor, and Aaron Downey, project editor, who guided me through the process of sharing my thinking. Thanks also to my copyeditor, Kate Petrella.

One of my favorite memories from childhood is of Saturday mornings spent in our local library with my mom and brother and sisters. I remember the magic of story hour, the formality of the hushed rooms, staring up at shelves loaded with books that towered over my head, the exact location of my favorites, and trying to navigate myself out the doors and down the steps with a Dr. Seuss-like crooked stack piled in my arms. My dad and I now spend many similarly glorious Saturday afternoons browsing through our local bookstore. My mother and father instilled in my brother and sisters and me a love of reading that has fueled a lifelong commitment to learning. I thank them both for this gift.

My sister Cris has been my cheerleader, deadline checker, and the one person who would call and interrupt my writing just to be sure I was writing. (Of course, I was . . . just in case she called to check.) Thanks, Cris!

And Rick. I know that's not a sentence. There is no sentence that sums up a husband who is willing to put everything on hold while his wife writes a book. Thank you, Rick, for caring as much about children as I do, and believing that my work with them makes a difference.

Introduction

Conversation creates the conditions for us to rediscover
the joy of thinking together.
—Margaret Wheatley

It was the spring of our first year at the Professional Development Center. My first-graders and I had just wrapped up a nonfiction unit of study in reading in which we had immersed ourselves in the discovery of fascinating things in, and thoughts about, the real world. As part of the study, we spent time learning to use the features of the genre to support meaning-making. From there, we shifted into a character study in fiction, focusing on the importance of building an understanding of what's in a character's heart by listening to their words and carefully scrutinizing their actions. Embedded in these studies, as in all aspects of our learning, was the importance of thinking and talking about our thinking as a means of constructing ideas, negotiating meaning, and developing structures for independent thought.

I was walking in the door of the classroom, having just left the Professional Development Room, and bumped (literally) into Sergio, who was posted at the door, waiting for me. He had a book in his hand, and was bursting with excitement.

"Look, look!" he erupted. "This fish is dam selfish . . . see, it says right here—dam selfish!"

I stopped flat in my tracks to see what he was talking about. Sure enough, he had a nonfiction book about sharks filled with diagrams and charts. He was pointing to a drawing of a food chain, a part of which was a picture of a fish eating another fish's eggs. A *damselfish*, to be precise.

I went into teacher mode, explaining to him that this was a name of a fish, and it was a word with three chunks, or syllables, and the accent was on the first chunk, so it was pronounced **dam**-sel-fish, not dam-**selfish**.

Sergio's face scrunched up (as only a child totally engrossed in thought can), and he intently studied the drawing as he mulled over what I had said.

"No, no, Mrs. Nichols . . . ," he finally mused. "Me and Manny and Issy, we already talked about it. This fish is eating this other fish's eggs, and that's dam selfish!"

Ah, yes, Sergio had done what I had failed to do. He had integrated his non-fiction and fiction study, using these ways of thinking about text to carefully consider what was in a character's heart as he simultaneously made sense of a diagram, supported by purposeful talk with his peers. So goes the work of teaching children to think together and negotiate meaning!

Constructivist thinking like this does not happen by accident. It is the by-product of classrooms where children think and talk together to make meaning, work collectively to construct stronger ideas, push back at thinking that doesn't make sense to them (even the teacher's), come to expect and anticipate differences of opinion, and do this on such a regular basis that thinking in this way becomes a habit of mind.

In these classrooms, phrases such as "I don't get you!" "Wait, do you mean . . .?" and Sergio's "No, no . . . !" are not argumentative, but are genuine efforts to think, talk, and understand. They are the children's way of saying, "I don't quite understand or agree but I value your ideas, so let's keep thinking and talking about this." These phrases are the language of negotiating meaning.

Yet, how much time do we devote in our instructional day to teaching children to think and talk about their thinking as a means of constructing ideas and negotiating meaning? How much time do we spend helping children to understand the power that comes from listening to the thoughts of others, and together building a greater understanding than we were able to attain individually? Do we help our children to experience and value conversation as a tool to build meaning of a text, and as a tool for taking these ideas and applying them to our world?

Creating classrooms where children think and talk purposefully is not easy. But, too, it is never boring . . . and never a day goes by that I'm not amazed at how brilliant children can be as a result!

The Importance of Developing the Ability to Think and Talk in Today's World

By changing the way we talk, we change the way we think,
not just as individuals, but all together.

—William Isaacs

KENNY: Ew—it's a beetle?
SERGIO: Dung beetle.
KENNY: What's that?
SERGIO: I think it's a *kind* of beetle—wait—here. See—dung—it's what they eat.
KENNY: They eat what? Dung? What's that? Keep reading . . .

AMBER: It's Abe when he was little. It says *When he was a boy* . . .
JOSHUA: That *had* to be along time ago . . .

VANESSA: (studying picture of desert hare) So its ears are long to get cool?
L.G: Yeah, 'cuz the desert's so hot . . .

KENNY: Oh, that's messed up!

It's late September, and I'm taking a moment to watch and listen to my second- and third-graders, who are spread out around the classroom reading. I've developed a beginning sense of each—their strengths, ways of learning, and social abilities—and am already starting to imagine futures filled with possibilities.

Of course, the possibilities that I imagine for my children may not match their aspirations or those of their families. Where I see a Harvard M.B.A. or a Juilliard-trained soloist, there may actually be a spirit that moves in a very different direction. Knowing this, one of my goals must be to prepare these children for a future blessed with choice, an array of motivating, enriching options that arise from their ability to excel in the continuously evolving workplace.

And, what of the bigger world that will surround this workplace? Looking through a wider lens, I must hope that my children develop the sense of purpose, focus, and habits of mind needed to lend their voices to the continual reauthoring of our democratic way of life. In this way, no matter what their choice for the future, it will live inside a just and caring world.

What abilities, then, will our children need so that the possibilities of the future are open to them? In *Schools That Learn*, Peter Senge warns that, "No one really knows what the working world, or indeed, what civilization and culture worldwide will be like in eighteen years, when today's kindergarteners graduate from college" (2000, 10).

What we do know, though, is that the goals of the traditional model for education will not enable our children to succeed in the changing professional landscape or equip them to construct the understandings required to make sense of and live smartly within a vastly diverse yet increasingly interconnected world.

The Schools that Were

Our traditional model of schooling evolved for the purpose of preparing children for success in an industrial world. In this world, work was an individual effort, and many jobs required workers to complete a task that produced but a small piece of the whole. Workers did not need to think, just do. Thinking and understanding the bigger picture was the boss' purview.

The learning processes in traditional models for school mimicked the individualistic, passive inclination of the industrial workplace. Teachers filled silent children with deposits of information in what Paulo Freire characterized as a banking model of instruction. "Education thus becomes an act of depositing, in which the students are the depositories and the teacher is the depositor. Instead of communicating, the teacher issues communiqués and makes deposits, which the students patiently receive, memorize, and repeat" (2003, 72). Freire rejected this banking model as a manifestation of an elite and oppressive segment of society.

David Perkins, whose research includes quantifying the result of this one-way, authoritative transmission of information from teacher to student, refers to the result as the "Trivial Pursuit" model of education (1992). He attributes the model to the naive but widely accepted theory that knowledge is an accumulation of facts and routines.

To understand why a pedagogy that honors silence and conformity will not enable children of today to flourish in the world of tomorrow, we must listen to the voices of those who are blazing the paths toward the new economy, and those who rally us to continuously engage in the process that shapes our democratic way of life.

Voices from the New Economy

Today's business gurus honor the knowledge that resides in their employees as the new competitive resource. Peter Senge, one visionary of this new, knowledge-based economy, argues that "the working world is no longer looking for 'industrial workers.' Employers of tomorrow likely will place a much higher value on listening and communication skills, on collaborative learning capabilities, and on critical thinking and systems thinking skills because most work is increasingly interdependent, dynamic and global" (2000, 51). Teams have replaced the individual as the foundation of effective organizations, and the work is no longer simple, isolated tasks.

In *The Art of Focused Conversation*, R. Brian Stanfield speaks of these ongoing changes in the workplace, emphasizing the increased demand for communication, conversation, and participation of all members of an organization. What's required, it seems, is not just chatter, but focused conversation; purposeful, in-depth talk that allows ideas to develop, and to "keep the intellectual capital of the organization flowing from all corners and departments" (2000, 20).

This concept of organizational intelligence in a new, knowledge-based economy is founded on the realization that no one person in the workplace has the entirety of knowledge required to do a given job. Rather, successful organizations will rely on the collective intelligence of people who are adept at thinking together. It seems that the changing business world is not as interested in the Trivial Pursuit champ as they are in individuals who know how to use their knowledge and the knowledge of their coworkers in constructive ways to problem solve.

Perkins reflects this belief in *King Arthur's Round Table: How Collaborative Conversations Create Smart Organizations* (2003). Perkins views this collective intelligence as predictive of an organization's success, observing that "How smart an organization or community is reflects the kinds of conversations people have with one another" (2003, 14).

To support the necessary transition from individual to collective effort, Peter Senge points to dialogue as the most effective tool. William Isaacs, author of *Dialogue: The Art of Thinking Together* (1999), agrees, asserting, "Dialogue seeks to harness the 'collective intelligence' . . . of the people around you; together we are more aware and smarter than we are on our own" (11).

I happened upon the perfect illustration of collective intelligence while flipping between T.V. stations one evening. An unusual phrase, "aggressive runway," hooked me into an episode of *Modern Marvels*. An *aggressive* runway? The term, it turns out, was being used to describe the runway for the space shuttle at Kennedy Space Center in Florida. To create a shuttle runway that would perform in Florida's rainy climate, the researchers at NASA's Langley Research Center formulated a surface with deep transverse grooves and a rough surface. It was great for wet-weather landings, but devastating for the shuttle tires. The "aggressive runway" actually wore the tires down to their internal structure, creating potentially dangerous situations.

The researchers at Langley needed to pinpoint the tipping point between a runway surface that would handle the weight and velocity of the space shuttle on landing and prevent skidding in wet conditions, but without causing tire damage beyond a degree of acceptable risk. Imagine the experiments, the trials, the failures and successes, and above all, the conversations! I find myself smiling in awe as I imagine individuals with knowledge of tire structure, surface design, and space shuttle engineering engaged in purposeful conversation for the purpose of problem-solving in a novel situation. The answer was not simply a function of combining their knowledge, but instead lay in using their combined knowledge to create new knowledge. I don't think I'll ever watch a shuttle landing the same way again!

This ability to construct ideas with others through purposeful talk, or dialogue, is essential. In his foreword to *Crucial Conversations: Tools for Talking When the Stakes Are High* (Patterson et al., 2002), Stephen R. Covey speaks of this give-and-take effort used when we think and talk for the purpose of reaching consensus or problem solving. "These newer, better solutions will not represent 'my way' or 'your way'—they will represent 'our way.' In short, the solutions must be synergistic, meaning that the whole is greater than the sum of the parts" (2002, xii). As David Perkins explains, collaborative efforts in novel situations reflect "how effectively the members exchange and pool ideas and sift possibilities; how progressive their conversations are." Perkins quotes colleague Ernesto Gore, who put it succinctly when he said, "Organizations are made of conversations" (Perkins, 2003).

Let's hold up this value the professional world is placing on conversations against the results of a banking model of instruction and "Trivial Pursuit" view of intelligence. Will children who grow up intellectually in such classrooms develop the ability to engage in purposeful talk with the goal of creating knowledge in collaboration with others? The message the business world is sending is clear: We need to rethink the desired end result of a public school education.

Voices for a Democratic Society

Public schools do not exist for the sole purpose of supporting the workplace, however. The American philosopher John Dewey believed that a "political education" took precedence over other purposes of public education in a democratic society. Dewey asserted that, to create and sustain progressive democratic ways of life, people must have opportunities to learn what a democratic way of life entails, and how to live in these ways (1916).

In *For a Better World: Reading and Writing for Social Action*, author/educators Randy and Katherine Bomer observe that "Democracy is not what we have when the process is over: it exists only when people deliberate together" (2001, 14). Essentially, democracy is a verb. Constructive conversations, often difficult and messy in nature, are the essence of this way of living together.

Paulo Freire agrees, arguing that education should be the purveyor of critical thinking and creativity, both of which enable participation in and the continual re-creation of a participatory system of democracy. Schools, he asserts, should create critical, "unquiet" minds. "Banking education resists dialogue; problem posing education regards dialogue as indispensable to the act of cognition which unveils reality" (83). In other words, it is through purposeful talk with others that we construct ideas and visions of possibility for ourselves and each other. Peter Johnston refers to this constructive thinking and talking curriculum as the "literacy of democracy" (1997, 77).

Margaret Wheatley, a respected organizational thinker, takes a holistic view of these conversations, seeing them as a means of restoring hope and cultivating the conditions necessary for change. In *Turning to One Another: Simple Conversations to Restore Hope to the Future* (2002), Wheatley encourages us to slow down our lives, and find time for both purposeful conversation with others and reflective conversation with ourselves. She worries about the rarity of this in today's world, noting that, "Some of us have never been invited to share our ideas and opinions. From early school days and now as adults, we've been instructed to be quiet so others can tell us what to think" (24).

Again, we need to ask ourselves if the traditional model of education creates the habits of mind needed to think critically, and the ability to engage in purposeful talk as members of a participatory democracy. Can children who are trained to passively and unquestioningly absorb information in isolation become the new generative force behind an evolving democratic way of life?

Purposeful Talk Defined

I was book shopping online recently, and, on an impulse, typed in the word *conversation*. That one word brought up 86,610 titles. This alone alludes to the developing importance of conversation in our increasingly complex world. While I admit to tiring of my search after several hundred titles, most of the texts I scrolled past looked at talk as a tool that helps us to relate to the world at both the personal and the professional level. From organizational leadership and change to honest communication with those who matter most to us, the capacity to engage in conversation with others is undeniably an admired and valuable ability.

Yet, the prevailing mindset for conversation in today's world is one of people engaged in casual chitchat. In casual conversation, we follow loosely connected strings of ideas with no particular focus other than enjoyment of a personal interchange. Or worse, we use the guise of conversation to spew forth a dissertation of our own ideas simply to validate ourselves. In both scenarios, ideas or information may be communicated, but there is no intent to work with the information constructively beyond the exchange.

If we are to prepare our children for a world that is propelled by purposeful conversations and collective intelligence, teaching them to communicate well at the chitchat level, or likewise to talk "at" others rather than "with" others, will not suffice. In his essay "On Dialogue," David Bohm (1996) distinguishes between the act of communicating and that of dialogue. Communication, he explains, is a telling of one's ideas, making one's thinking clear to another. But dialogue, he continues, is a coming to an intellectual exchange willing to see and hear something new in the exchange, and actually creating a newer, stronger understanding because of the exchange. Dialogue, as Bohm defines it, is a true negotiation of meaning (1996, 2). Through this constructive process, participants achieve a whole that is greater than the sum of its parts—ideas that are bigger and better than any individual might have conceived on their own. William Isaacs agrees with this definition, stating, "Dialogue . . . is about a shared inquiry, a way of thinking and reflecting together" (1999, 9).

In his book *Life in a Crowded Place*, Ralph Peterson also differentiates among various types of oral communication, including conversation, discussion, and dialogue. While all three forms of communication have their place in classrooms, Peterson aligns conversation and discussion with more casual social encounters. But dialogue, Peterson argues, is a special kind of talk, wherein constructing meaning becomes the primary focus. "In dialogue, we attempt to call forth the best the other person has to offer and put forth the best we can imagine. Dialogue requires thoughtful listening and responding. It is a time when participants collaborate and co-produce meaning. Where learning is concerned, I believe the kind of talk to be prized above all others is dialogue" (1992, 104).

Dialogue, then, is separated from other forms of conversation by purpose, and it is this purposefulness with talk that we want to instill in our children. For this very reason, I refer to the way I converse with my colleagues and children, and teach children to converse and learn with others, as purposeful talk.

Voices from Education

Clearly, the path toward creating a future filled with opportunity and choice for our children is paved with the ability to think and talk with others in purposeful ways as a means of generating ideas and constructing understanding.

Russian psychologist Lev Vygotsky proposed a social development theory of learning, in which social interaction in the form of dialogue plays a fundamental role in cognitive development. Vygotsky asserts that learning best occurs when the learner engages in purposeful talk; a negotiation of meaning, with a learned other in the Zone of Proximal Development (1978, 84–91). This challenges traditional teaching models, necessitating an environment and instructional design that allows teachers and children to collaborate with each other.

In "What I've Learned About Effective Reading Instruction," published in the June 2002 issue of the *Phi Delta Kappan*, Richard Allington outlines findings from his research with colleague Peter Johnston in exemplary teachers' classrooms. Allington describes 6 Ts, or common features, of effective elementary literacy instruction. Not surprisingly, the second T is talk. Allington highlights vast differences in the quality and quantity of talk between classrooms with highly effective teachers and those with more traditional teachers (740–747).

In the traditional classroom, teacher talk dominates, while silent children are expected to absorb. Hands are raised to speak, usually in response to the teacher's questions. Literal answers formulated by single learners are accepted as evidence of comprehension. In highly effective teachers' classrooms, however, talk is modeled and taught throughout the year. This talk has a conversational tone and flow as opposed to a controlled, interrogational pattern. Children are encouraged to use talk as a tool to engage with others' ideas and construct hypotheses, strategies, and concepts.

Research conducted by The Institute for Learning, an entity created through a partnership between The Learning Research and Development Center of the University of Pittsburgh and school districts nationwide, resulted in a set of core beliefs, or principles, known collectively as The Principles of Learning (Resnick, 1999, 38–40). These principles are intended to guide teachers and educational systems toward creating a curriculum of thoughtfulness and improving instruction for all children.

One of these core beliefs, "Accountable Talk," closely echoes definitions of dialogue from the business world and encourages teachers toward the quantity and quality of talk that Allington and Johnston found in exceptional classrooms. In *Reading and Writing Grade by Grade* (1999), the New Standards Primary Literacy Committee boldly states that "Accountable talk is not empty chatter; it seriously responds to and further develops what others in the group say. Students introduce and ask for knowledge that is accurate and relevant to the text under discussion. They use evidence from the text in ways that are appropriate and follow established norms of good reasoning" (25).

Purposeful, or "accountable" talk then, by definition, has both a process and a purpose. Accountable talk is not something children do for a specified period of time during the day, but a way of being present and focused in a learning environment, a way of living as a learner. It requires learners to "keep their head in the game," think, and give voice to their thinking with the understanding that participating in talk allows them to construct and negotiate meaning. Children are accountable to themselves and to the other learners they are engaged with. These learners depend on each other's thinking to enrich their understanding and construct meaning.

In *Classroom Discourse: The Language of Teaching and Learning*, Courtney Cazden places extraordinary value on talk, stating that "the basic purpose of school is achieved through communication" (2001, 2). A coauthor of *Reading and Writing Grade by Grade* (1999), Cazden strengthens the argument for accountable, or purposeful talk, by highlighting the limits of lessons utilizing the Initiate/Response/Evaluate pattern of classroom talk now widely documented in American classrooms.

Derived from the "Trivial Pursuit" definition of knowledge, teachers using the Initiate/Response/Evaluate pattern ask "display," or inauthentic questions, to test individual children's acquisition of facts. A correct response is met with teacher approval, while an incorrect response is most often dismissed with a shake of the head or a proclamation of "incorrect" as the teacher moves on to someone else. As an alternative, Cazden proposes a shift toward learning communities that use purposeful talk to initiate their own problems and questions, explore possibilities, and construct and negotiate meaning together.

Children do not need, nor can they afford, to wait until high school or beyond to learn to use talk in purposeful ways. Deep into our third year at the Professional Development Center, three of my second- and third-graders were reading *Mrs. Katz and Tush*, by Patricia Polacco. Manny, Anthony, and Issy were contemplating the complex behavior of Mrs. Katz when she visited her deceased husband in the cemetery. Their conversation illustrates the process of thinking and talking together for the purpose of constructing meaning. Let's listen in.

Issy: Why does Mrs. Katz do that when she goes there . . . to that . . . the . . .
Anthony: Cement . . . cemetery?
Issy: Yeah, the cemetery. Why does she read and put a rock on it—on the stone?
Manny: I think it's how they do stuff, like their way from long ago.
Anthony: (Looking confused) I don't get you!
Manny: OK, well, let's just say I was married to someone. I'm not, but let's just say I was. Then, we would always do things the same just 'cuz we're married. So, Mrs. Katz keeps doing that stuff 'cuz her husband would get it.
Issy: Oh, so it's like remembering together.
Anthony: Yeah, even though one of them is gone! But now, she's teaching Larnel.
Issy: But why?
Manny: It probably makes her feel better.
Anthony: But she's crying, so I don't think she feels better.

Issy: But Anthony, maybe it makes her feel better because, because, he—her husband—he would know she's doing it. It's like Manny said, it's their . . . it's their long-ago way.

Anthony: Oh, so, you're saying . . . yeah, I think it could, maybe she does feel better if he would know. Maybe it's like keeping him in her heart. And now, Larnel will know, too.

Manny: Yeah, I think . . . that's why she does it!

As Bohm suggests, these children allow their thoughts to flow, rather than trying to persuade or convince each other. While persuasive abilities are an unmistakably valuable element of proficient language use, as well as an effective tool for success in the world, it is this open-minded yet purposeful dialogue that enables the construction of deeper meaning. And, it is the cumulative effect of daily conversations such as this that will create the habits of mind that enable strong thinking even when constructing meaning alone. What if we began in kindergarten teaching children to learn through constructive conversations with others? Imagine the sound of a third-grade or sixth-grade class of children who have been thinking and negotiating meaning through purposeful talk since kindergarten!

The following chapters will focus on supporting children in building richly literate lives while simultaneously developing the conversational and constructive abilities using purposeful talk that will generate options in our complex and changing world. In this text, this work will be focused in the reading workshop, but ultimately, we want children to understand that purposeful talk is not just about reading; it is the essence of learning. It is a vehicle for the construction of knowledge, a valued means of navigating the professional world, the process by which our democratic way of life was forged, and our hope for its continued success.

The Interconnectedness of Language Development and Purposeful Talk

Language exerts hidden power, like a moon on the tides.
—Rita Mae Brown

SHERINNE: I think he's (the author) trying to say that, when the soldiers first came, they made a big crowd. They made the colonists say 'Whoa! Where'd you come from?'

JIOVANNI: They mad because they (the colonists) don't want him (pointing to soldiers) come here.

RONNIE: Yeah, so then I have one question. Why did the colonists even let them arrive in their harbor?

JIOVANNI: (smiles and nods)

TYREESE: They don't know war's gonna happen or nothing!

In classrooms across the United States, coast to coast and everywhere in between, we encounter inquisitive, eager children thinking and talking to make meaning of their world, and drawing on a range of proficiency with the English language to do so. This snippet of talk emerged during Shared Reading as Stephanie Hasselbrink's fifth-grade class at Webster Elementary, an inner-city school in San Diego, worked to construct meaning of a text titled "Lobsterbacks" from *Liberty! How the Revolutionary War Began* by Lucille Recht Penner.

The children were studying the way readers draw on their strategies for making meaning of fiction text when reading in other genres. Specifically, they were thinking about characters and their interplay with setting as the class read, thought, and talked together to understand historical nonfiction. The children were considering the British soldiers' interactions with the colonists, and working to understand them in light of the way of the world at the time. Their talk creates for us a snapshot of the rich array of language learners and users so typical in our classrooms, and highlights the importance of developing an ability in all children to communicate with clarity.

Language and Purposeful Talk

We are inexplicably drawn to people who have a way with words. Their thoughts seem to be dressed in an alluring mix of power and poetry that compels us to listen. The authors of *Speaking and Listening for Preschool Through Third Grade* not only agree, but add a serious twist. "People who listen, speak, and use language well are more likely to succeed in their purposes than people who struggle to express themselves" (2001, 25).

Clearly, our children's ability with language affects every aspect of their academic lives and beyond. Notably, those with a richly developed language system are better able to think in complex ways, understand complex ideas, and give voice to their thinking. In addition, a well-developed ability with language enables more thought-provoking purposeful talk.

Language development and purposeful talk are beautifully intertwined. As we work to grow one stronger, our capacity for the other follows suit. The authors of the First Steps Oral Language Developmental Curriculum, authored by the Education Department of Western Australia, believe that "Purposeful talk is one of the major means through which children construct and refine their understandings of language" (1994, 14). When our children learn inside a constructivist curriculum that draws on talk as a tool, they are constantly challenged to think and give voice to their thinking as they negotiate and construct meaning. It is this process of negotiating and constructing meaning that pushes children to work at the cutting edge of their ability with language and propels them forward as English language learners.

 ## All Children Are Language Learners

Let's briefly consider the language abilities that enabled our fifth-graders to explore the arrival of the Redcoats. Both Sherinne and Ronnie are developing strength with language, showing an awareness of audience and an ability to express their thinking with clarity. Jiovanni is new to English, and employs a mix of oral language and gestures to make sure his goal of communicating his thinking is accomplished, showing joy when he knows he has succeeded. Tyreese's point is clear and shows evidence of confident, decisive thinking, which is undiluted by the less formal syntax and vocabulary.

These four, along with the others in the class, had sufficient language to construct a stronger meaning than any one of them might have accomplished on their own. Yet, to continue to grow in their ability to engage in purposeful talk for a wide range of purposes, including negotiating and constructing meaning of increasingly complex text and of their world, all four of these children must continue to grow as language learners and users.

Although our early years are the richest for language development, language learning is a progression that continues throughout our lives. The *First Steps Oral Language Developmental Continuum*, a framework that assists teachers with assessing, teaching, and monitoring oral language development, identifies eight phases of development, from beginning language use to an advanced ability, which stretches into adulthood. Even as adults, we continuously fine-tune our ability to control the subtle nuances of language as we master the art of communicating with a range of audiences for a range of purposes in a range of contexts. Our goal is a sophisticated understanding of the power and effect of spoken language, which includes the ability to use language to express, reshape, and clarify thinking; to use a wide variety of language forms; to manipulate language to suit a range of audiences, purposes and situations; to monitor and control language with confidence, and to manipulate words effectively as situations require.

The First Steps continuum is based on an overall pattern of language development for native speakers, and focuses on language children need for success in academic situations and "in contexts that society judges essential for success"

(1994, 15). In addition to speech development, which tracks grammar, phonics, and syntax, the continuum focuses on language development for participation in social situations, as a support for reading and writing, and as a vehicle for thought. Table 2–1 highlights a sampling of the key indicators of phases 3–8.

Likewise, the New Standards Speaking and Listening Committee's *Speaking and Listening for Preschool Through Third Grade* (2001) were created using a synthesis of research focusing on language abilities needed to succeed academically. Language development is tracked through the lenses of:

◆ habit: children's need and willingness to talk a lot
◆ kinds of talk and resulting genres: children's ability to talk for a variety of purposes
◆ language and conventions: children's progression with the social and grammatical rules of language, and a rich vocabulary

The categories and descriptors of behavior from these documents support our ability to assess a child's progress with constructing and communicating meaning through language, and suggest areas of instructional emphasis that will strengthen thinking, communication, and the construction of meaning through purposeful talk.

Creating the Conditions that Enable Language Learning

Australian researcher Brian Cambourne identified eight conditions that create the optimal social and emotional environment for learning. Originally observed during and proposed for language learning, the conditions are now widely recognized as creating ideal circumstances for literacy learning in general. These interconnected conditions, known as The Conditions for Learning, are based on the belief that learning is a natural and social process (1988).

Ideally, The Conditions for Learning should permeate all classrooms to support successful literacy development. In classrooms where purposeful talk flourishes, Cambourne's Conditions for Learning thrive as well. They are created as we teach children to think and talk as a tool for constructing meaning, and in turn encourage children to participate more fully in purposeful talk. Table 2–2 illustrates this reciprocal nature between the Conditions for Learning and Purposeful Talk.

A Sampling of Key Indicators from The First Steps Oral Language Continuum (1994)

	Phase 3: Exploratory Language	Phase 4: Emergent Language for Learning	Phase 5: Consolidated Language for Learning	Phase 6: Extended Language for Learning	Phase 7: Proficient Language Use	Phase 8: Advanced Language Use
Language of Social Interaction	• Contributes to classroom interactions, and is aware of and indicates lack of understanding	• Enhances meaning by using appropriate volume, pacing, intonation, and gestures • Considers audience and purpose • Sustains conversation	• Communicates effectively by sharing ideas, offering advice, opinion, and information • Reacts to contributions of others	• Selects and sustains language and styles to match purpose, context and audience • Successfully interprets whether message has been understood	• Uses language purposefully to include or exclude others	• Shows a sophisticated understanding of the power and effect of spoken language
Language and Literacy	• Retells with adequate details, including who, what, when, where	• Is developing specific vocabulary for specific purposes • Shows evidence of sustained, logical conversation	• Adapts language to purpose and context • Uses language to develop topics • Interprets texts from own point of view • Uses academic language	• Summarizes main ideas, draws conclusions from, infers and evaluates written and oral texts • Describes topics outside immediate experience • Listens and responds to other perspectives	• Uses language critically to reflect on and analyze spoken and written text • Uses text structures and language features confidently based on purpose, context, and audience in cooperation with peers	• Interacts responsibly, critically and confidently in a variety of contexts for a variety of purposes • Matches approach and language to context and audience
Language and Thinking	• Uses language to explain, ask, and compare	• Uses language to predict and recall • Uses language as a tool for interacting with others to achieve a purpose	• Developing ability to reason and think logically	• Uses language to express independent critical thinking, formulate hypotheses, criticize, evaluate, plan, and influence others	• Uses language to reflect on learning and construct understanding	• Analyzes spoken texts from familiar and unfamiliar contexts critically

Table 2–1

The reciprocal nature of Cambourne's Conditions for Learning and the Ability to Participate in Purposeful Talk	
→ → → **Cambourne's Conditions** ← ← ←	→ → → **Purposeful Talk** ← ← ←
Immersion: Learners need to be immersed in the content they are acquiring.	As children talk freely and continuously throughout the day, they are immersed in both language and the power of talk as a constructivist tool.
Demonstration: Learners need many opportunities to hear and see and understand what is expected in a variety of contexts.	Children have multiple daily opportunities to observe the teacher and peers as models of proficient, purposeful talk.
Engagement: Learners must believe they are thinkers, speakers, and meaning makers, and participate actively.	Through immersion in and demonstration of talk, children develop a desire to engage and a belief that they can.
Expectation: Learner, teacher, and peers must believe that success is possible.	The social nature of purposeful talk ensures support and response, which creates a sense of agency.
Responsibility: Learners must make decisions and hold themselves and others accountable to gain independence.	Children are in charge of their own role in purposeful talk, and are responsible for engaging to express an idea or elicit more information. All children expect support from each other in the meaning-making process.
Use: Learners need time and opportunity to engage in meaningful contexts.	Purposeful talk permeates the day, and is used to construct real understandings about our world.
Approximation: Learners need to be allowed to be risk takers and learn from mistakes.	Conversational responses from others allow children to notice and rethink errors without judgment.
Response: Learners need feedback from knowledgeable others.	Conversational responses from others allow children to gauge their success with communicating their ideas.

Table 2–2

This reciprocal relationship ensures that children who use talk as a tool are continuously refining their ability with language, which in turn enables stronger talk. The result is an ever-increasing ability to converse purposefully and construct deeper meaning.

 ## Language Learners Needing Added Support

The range of language learners in classrooms across the country includes children new to English, and children whose native language is English, but whose development is noticeably different or delayed.

Nonnative English Speakers

Our children new to English may come from around the world, or from around the corner. They may be newcomers to the United States, or native-born Americans who have been sheltered in culturally and linguistically homogeneous neighborhoods. They come to us with a variety of facility with their native language, and a variety of educational backgrounds.

One typically scorching late summer day in San Diego, Staci Wright headed off toward the upper grade wing at Webster Elementary with a line of fourth-graders, anxious to catch a first glimpse of their new classroom.

"Hey, look—two tubs of mysteries! And the Cinderella tales!"

"Yea, and there's Cynthia Rylant over here!"

"Hey—look! Science stuff! Whoa—an aquarium! What is it? A snake? No—a turtle?"

"Where do you think you'll sit?"

In the midst of the joy and anticipation, indistinguishable from the others, is Abdi. Describing Abdi as indistinguishable, at least for the moment, is to speak volumes about his progress as a third-grader in Jeralyn Treas' class last year.

Abdi and his family are Bantu from Somali. They lived in a refugee camp in Kenya before coming to the United States. Abdi entered Webster Elementary at the tail end of second grade knowing little more than a few phrases of English. His first true immersion into classroom culture and the English language was the start of his third-grade year with Jeralyn. His early days in this vibrant community were lived in a serious, studious silence. At least, Abdi was silent on the outside. I have no doubt that his head was filled with raging conversations as he watched, listened, and worked to make meaning in his new surroundings.

Had Abdi landed in a classroom where children were anchored to single desks, only speaking to propose precise, correct answers, he would have had very little to watch, listen to, and study. But, not so! In just a year's time, Abdi's English language developed well enough to enable him to follow and participate in conversation, ask questions, agree and disagree, and share complete and complex ideas, all with his trademark studious seriousness. Although much of this success speaks to Abdi's determination to learn, a considerable degree of his success also stems from being immersed in a classroom of children who put purposeful talk at the heart of their learning.

Native English Speakers with Different Developmental Patterns

Thomas bounced up the ramp and into our second/third-grade class at the Professional Development Center one day a few weeks into the year. Thomas had an infectious, eager smile, seemed to thoroughly enjoy coming to school, and displayed all the surface behaviors of one engaged in meaningful learning. He would sit quietly for long periods of time engrossed in books, which he decoded with few errors. He sat attentively during Read Aloud, looked right at the speaker during conversations, smiled when the other children smiled, and in general seemed to be a confident child.

Thomas's records indicated English as his first and only language. But after working with Thomas for just a few days, it was obvious that something was amiss. His talk indicated he did not always understand class conversations, and discussions about his reading revealed confusions, even at the literal level. His ability to communicate was often hampered by his syntactical construction of English, and word-choice errors.

A meeting with Thomas's mom helped me to understand his language needs. Mom, a single parent who had learned English as a second language, did not speak to Thomas in her native language, because she wanted him to learn English. Her English was limited, with a still-developing syntactic structure and narrow range of vocabulary. This was the model of language Thomas was immersed in at home, and which shaped his language system.

The research of Hart and Risley, explored in their book *Meaningful Differences in the Everyday Experiences of Young American Children* (1995) gives us a peek into the home lives of children from a range of socioeconomic backgrounds. By sharing data and talk transcripts, the authors illustrate vast differences in the quantity and quality of language in which children are immersed during their early years. The authors concluded that not all children have the advantage of growing up in an environment that develops a rich facility with language. A lack of a language-rich environment may be due to stress in the home, specific communication or parenting styles, a lack of fluent language models as with Thomas, a lack of fluent adult speakers who interact with the child frequently, and most notably, relative economic advantage.

Thomas's confident nature and his understanding of the social components of conversation proved to be invaluable strengths as we worked to support him in his efforts to communicate. Expressing for Thomas our interest in his ideas, responding to and supporting him as he found the words to convey his thinking, modeling the structures needed to phrase the ideas, and building his vocabulary were all part of involving Thomas in purposeful talk. Like Abdi, once he knew he was surrounded by peers who cared, valued his thinking, and would support his efforts, Thomas put his full energy into communicating, and grew stronger as a result.

Working with children such as Thomas and Abdi may have us initially thinking that a curriculum of talk is not appropriate. Yet, their struggles with expressing their thinking cannot be construed as a reason to avoid purposeful talk. To the contrary, it is all the more reason why we must create opportunities for all children to talk purposefully and often.

In *When Students Have Time to Talk: Creating Contexts for Learning Language*, authors Dudley-Marling and Searle insightfully suggest that "classrooms have the potential to be the ideal language-learning environments because they can offer a range of things to talk about, reasons for talking, and an audience for talk" (1991, viii). For our classrooms to become true language labs, we must immerse all children in motivating, meaning-based experiences that will engage them at the edge of their linguistic competence. Simply said, "oral language development cannot be a spectator sport." (New Standards Speaking and Listening Committee, 2001, 14).

Supporting All Language Learners

As we design instruction that utilizes purposeful talk as a constructivist mechanism, it is reasonable to assume that all children will need some degree of support to continue developing their abilities with language. It also is crucial to recognize that many children, and not just those officially identified, will need thoughtful scaffolds. Our responsibility with all of our children is to bridge the gap between their current ability with English and the proficiency required for success in using language to construct and communicate increasingly complex meaning.

The following supports and strategies will enable you to create an environment and design instruction that enables all children to grow as thinkers, language users, and participants in purposeful talk. These should not be considered as add-ons, but as scaffolds or ways of learning that can be seamlessly woven into ongoing instruction.

Grouping

While it's true that offering ample opportunities to talk for meaningful purposes throughout the day is a crucial component for accelerating children's thinking, meaning-making, and language development, whole group talk is not the most effective grouping choice for all children all of the time. Many of our children need numerous small group opportunities for their learning to achieve its fullest potential.

Small group work ensures that children will have opportunities to talk and construct meaning with others, without being overpowered by their more language-proficient peers. In small group, children often develop confidence by taking risks they would not take in whole group situations. As children take risks and realize that, with the support of the teacher and others in the group, they are able to communicate their thinking and construct meaning, they begin to speak more often. This increased communication with support strengthens their ability with language, which in turn enables them to engage more fully in future conversations.

Even children seemingly quite fluent with English benefit from small group support as they work to acquire increasingly sophisticated nuances with language, such as negotiating for turns, or using language in subtle ways to persuade. Again, the small group structure offers more time for the children to engage in extended, supported talk with others.

Not all teachers use the same configuration of grouping at any given time due to differing language and academic needs in their classrooms. While whole group instruction is most often the springboard for our Reading Workshop, the talk curriculum, content curriculum, and strategies discussed throughout this book are appropriate for small group instruction as well.

Carefully Selected Partnerships

Reading Partnerships, which are discussed at length in Chapter 7, offer children a listener who cares about, supports, and responds to them and their message. Partnerships are most often used as a scaffold for that last leap between teacher-supported instruction and independence as we move thinking, talking, and meaning-making down the Release of Responsibility slide (see Figure 5–1 in Chapter 5). They may also be used for turn-and-talks, a support structure for whole class or small group conversation that is discussed in depth in Chapter 5.

Recently, a group of Webster teachers and I had the privilege of visiting Central Elementary in San Diego City Schools, where administrator Staci Monreal and a thoughtful, energetic staff are making tremendous strides with a population of children who are approximately eighty percent nonnative English language speakers. While there, we delighted in watching Alison Vinci and her third-graders as they studied fiction text to determine the effect of dialogue on meaning-making. After a minilesson that included teacher modeling, the children worked in partnerships to think and generate conversation. Then, Alison called the partners back to the carpet for whole group conversation. Before starting the conversation, Alison smartly had her children turn to their partners one last time to think about what they wanted to say and practice verbalizing the idea.

As the children began sharing and constructing in whole group, partners supported each other in communicating their ideas. Alison worked to orchestrate the talk, provide language support, clarify the idea if necessary, and offer feedback. Used in this way, the partnerships created an additional opportunity for extra rehearsal and acted as a scaffold during the actual construction of meaning. This added layer built confidence in all the children, and was crucial for those needing stronger language support.

When pairing more fluent speakers with children needing more language support, the right choice makes all the difference. An extremely talkative partner will dominate, not allowing the less proficient child ample talk time. Our quickest, strongest students may not have the patience for someone who requires more time to make meaning and express their thinking in English. Rather, children with caring personalities who are able to both coax and coach language use are often the best for the job.

Charting

As children think and talk to construct meaning, we chart their efforts as a visual representation, recording strategies for the purpose of encouraging and supporting future efforts, and eventually independence. Chapter 7 explores the role charting plays in moving purposeful talk down the Release of Responsibility slide.

In addition to supporting conversational moves and reminding children to think strategically, charting has the added advantage of creating a record of the language used in the process. As we chart during our Units of Study, which are explored in Chapter 6, we record key phrases and vocabulary, often referred to as academic language, including terms for and phrases used when discussing story elements, themes, features of text, text structures, and critical thinking, among others.

Children needing language support will draw from the language on the chart, using it to enable precise communication or to support their efforts to express their thoughts in English. To serve as language supports, charts need to be modeled as such, and be posted in visually accessible spots in the classroom.

Using Picture Books

Throughout the chapters to come, you will notice that the majority of the texts used in lessons are picture books. In picture books, gorgeous, lively pictures or photographs offer an added layer of support beyond the written text for meaning-making.

During whole group Read Alouds, Jeralyn smartly placed Abdi to her right side and two other children needing added language support to her left. As she read, she would tilt the book to each side as the children leaned in close, and point out details in the pictures before showing them to the whole class.

During a second read of *Buffalo Woman*, a complex Native American legend by Paul Goble, Abdi listened and looked on as Jeralyn pointed out details. As conversation began to build, Abdi's head moved from the picture to the other speakers and back. Slowly he raised his hand. Jeralyn immediately supported his effort to gain entry into the conversation. "What are you thinking, Abdi?" The other children leaned in to hear Abdi's soft voice and lend support.

"This is buffalo?" he asked, pointing to the picture of the animal.

"Yeah, that's it, the buffalo," his classmates encouraged.

"He say 'don't come' to boy—here." Abdi shared, pointing to the other character.

The support of the pictures was allowing Abdi greater clarity with the characters and events, and enabled him to construct understanding and communicate his thinking.

Multiple Exposures to Text

In our Reading Workshop, we often explore and construct meaning with a text over multiple reads, as discussed in Chapter 6. These multiple reads offer our nonnative English language learners and others needing added support opportunities to hear, make sense of, and try out new vocabulary and syntactical structures over a period of several days.

When possible, offering a small group or one-on-one read of a text prior to a whole group experience enables those needing this language support a chance to begin the process. While it is often difficult for the classroom teacher to find the time for this in a heavily impacted instructional day, perhaps creative options such as more language-proficient student-tutors or parent volunteers are a possibility.

Proximity

Jeralyn's careful placement of children needing more language support close to her ensured that she was not only able to share the visual supports in the text with them, but also whisper added bits of information to give them context. During turn-and-talks, Jeralyn would first lean over to her language learners and listen in to their talk, either to help get it started, or to assess the children's level of understanding. She was also better able to notice their efforts to join the conversation, and orchestrate their turn if necessary.

Expanding Vocabulary

To develop into skilled, mature conversationalists, we must learn enough words to keep the conversation lively and communicate subtle variations in meaning. Children who lack richly developed vocabulary are often unable to do either.

Some of our children simply need to learn English labels for words and concepts they already possess. However, many of our children require more sophisticated language to enable increasingly complex thinking and an ability to express that thinking. For instance, if words such as *happy* and *sad* are the limit of a child's ability to express feelings, how can they think about and express variations of those emotions, such as *exhilarated* or *miserable*?

Beck, McKeown, and Kucan, authors of *Bringing Words to Life: Robust Vocabulary Instruction,* view vocabulary as composed of three tiers. Tier-one words are common, basic words; tier-three are low frequency, topic, or content-specific words. The authors' contend that our focus for vocabulary development should be on the second tier, which consists of words that are "of high frequency for mature language users and are found across a variety of domains" (2002, 8). These tier-two words facilitate complex thought and allow us to communicate our ideas more precisely to others.

Texts offer meaningful contexts for conversations that stretch children's ability with language and allow us to introduce tier-two words. For example, as we discuss characters, their motives, and changes they undergo (ways of thinking explored in Chapter 6), we are able to introduce vocabulary that allows our children to understand and express a range of feelings and emotions. When conversation moves toward big ideas or the heart of the text, and the ways texts help us to think about issues in our world, we are again able to introduce vocabulary that expands children's thinking and ability to discuss real concepts and the complexities of life.

Beck, McKeown, and Kucan point out that to really know a word, a single exposure is not adequate. As we link conversations about topics or meaningful issues, we offer children multiple contexts in which to practice their newly acquired words.

Playfulness with words is another key aspect of learning vocabulary. After many discussions about characters that allowed us to explore new ways of expressing sadness, my children began trying to figure out which variation of *sad* was the *saddest.* They gathered words such as *heartbroken, blue, down, gloomy,* and *depressed,* among others. Then, they tried to organize them on a continuum from least sad to most sad. There was no right answer to all of this, but the talk about degrees of emotion couldn't be beat! And, what resulted was a group of children who never again said, "She's sad" when discussing a character, or real world people and events!

Another important component of vocabulary development is building children's ability to think and converse using academic language. Academic language includes not just content-specific terms and phrases, or tier-three words, but strategic language as well. Academic language enables children to communicate in precise ways, to discuss their thinking and learning process, and to converse smartly in more formal contexts beyond the world of school.

Digging into Topics over Time

As we explore the ways readers think, talk, and construct meaning with nonfiction, we make efforts to design our nonfiction studies around topics (see Chapter 6 for more in-depth information). Reading several texts on a single topic over time means that our children needing more language support are going to have multiple exposures to vocabulary associated with the topic and expanded opportunities to practice using it.

As they discuss the topic in greater depth, the children also develop a common language for discussing bigger issues surrounding the topic. As an example, fifth-graders reading, thinking, and talking about texts on steroid use not only learned medical and sports-related vocabulary but began to discuss and generate language for issues of personal choice and government control in our society. This language around bigger real-world issues then transferred to conversations about many different issues as the children's awareness grew.

Curt Dudley-Marling and Dennis Searle remind us that "by supporting and encouraging students to produce extended talk, we are allowing them to develop linguistic strategies that will make it possible for them to use language with increased effectiveness" (1991, 47). As students work collaboratively with others to construct meaning, they are motivated to speak and listen at the edge of their growing ability. As abilities with language improve, purposeful talk propels the construction of meaning to new dimensions.

Paradigm Shifts
What We're Pushing Away From, and Why

Children grow into the intellectual life around them.
—Lev Vygotsky

Before we turn our attention to creating classrooms where thinking and purposeful talk thrive, we need to discuss and dismantle some hallmarks of the "industrial model" of education. These hallmarks are beliefs about and conditions for teaching and learning that we tend to accept without question simply because they have "always been."

The following are beliefs and conditions that play particularly destructive roles in our attempts to develop purposeful talk. It is their omnipresence that makes these ways of living in academic environments the invisible saboteurs of our efforts. As we examine these beliefs and conditions, we must honestly ask ourselves if they continue to make sense within the context of our changing world, and then explore the evolution of thought around each.

From a Fixed View of Intelligence to Conditions that Enable Learned Intelligence

A group of fifth-graders and I were reading *The Unbreakable Code,* by Sara Hoagland Hunter (1996), the remarkable story of a grandfather who offers his grandson comfort and guidance through the story of his work as a Navajo Code Talker.

DeShawn: Hey, wait. I think it's not just about the boy. He's scared, but it's also about the grandfather. He talks about remembering Navajo, and that he'll never forget.
Alejandra: It's like proud. I think it's what this book is really about.
Maria: So, you're finding evidence of a possible theme?
Trevon: And it's only our first read. Man, we're getting smarter!

I couldn't have said it better! Indeed, this group of children had been immersed in studies that encouraged them to think and talk about text in increasingly complex ways, as well as in discussions of their own constructive process. Over time, their greater understanding of the constructive process enabled the children to think and talk about complex aspects of meaning with lessening support. They were learning how to learn. This ability is what David Perkins labels reflective intelligence (1995, 115).

Traditionalists believe that we are born with a set amount of intelligence that cannot be altered. It is this view of intelligence that supports the "banking model" of instruction. Fill the brain with as much as possible, test to see how much stuck, and grade based on this fixed ability to hold on to facts.

However, recent research on the human brain is providing a growing understanding of the workings of the brain and changing the way intelligence is defined. Researchers now view the brain as "a unique living organism that grows and reshapes itself in response to a challenge" (Abbott, 1997).

In his insightful text *Outsmarting I. Q.: The Emerging Science of Learnable Intelligence*, David Perkins explains this transition in thinking. To this end, he identifies three distinct kinds of intelligence:

◆ neural intelligence: what we are born with
◆ experiential intelligence: specialized knowledge acquired over time as a result of what we immerse ourselves in
◆ reflective intelligence: a combination of knowledge, understanding, and strategic ability (1995, 102–109)

While Perkins accepts that neural intelligence may well be fixed at birth, he contends that experiential and reflective intelligence can in fact be learned. Of greatest interest when creating classrooms that encourage thinking and purposeful talk is reflective intelligence.

Perkins asserts that reflective intelligence grows through instruction that cultivates metacognitive abilities and builds the strategies and attitudes conducive to good thinking. The more we talk purposefully about our thinking and take time to reflect on the process, the more efficiently and effectively we learn.

When children construct meaning by saying things like, "I'm thinking ___ because ___," they are making their thought process and the result of their process visible to others. Likewise, when we debrief a conversation through the lens of the constructed ideas and the process and strategies that allowed for the construction, children are able to rethink and gradually internalize the process. When we do this over and over every day in many contexts and content areas, habits of mind that enable intelligent behavior are formed.

Perkins speaks to the importance of a collective effort toward advancing reflective intelligence. "Intelligent behavior is not characteristically the solo dance of a naked brain, but an act that occurs in a somewhat supportive physical, social, and cultural context" (323).

Research from neuroscience supports this view of the brain as a social learner. In *Teaching with the Brain in Mind*, Eric Jensen tells us, "Essentially we are social beings and our brains grow in a social environment. Because we often forge meaning through socializing, the whole role of student-to-student discussions is vastly underused" (1998, 93). It seems that we learn to learn best when we think and talk with others.

The traditional model of passive learners memorizing and reciting does not allow for the constructive and reflective conversations necessary for the development of reflective intelligence. Research supports the shift not only toward purposeful talk that allows for the construction of ideas but also toward reflective conversations that focus on process and strategies.

From Individual Effort to Learning Communities

Of all the pieces we weave together to create classrooms where children read, think, and talk about their thinking to negotiate and construct meaning, the creation of a learning community is the most essential ingredient. One can have century-old single desks, achingly empty library shelves, and barely enough space for the class to gather, and still create a place where children read, think, and talk together to construct meaning *if* a true learning community exists.

There is something quite special about classrooms with a strong sense of community. To be in one is to be submerged in the pure joy of learning. These rooms have an aura of respect and shared purpose. Students know what they are doing and why, and they self-monitor their efforts and progress toward the goal.

In his pivotal book on developing community, Ralph Peterson reminds us that "in everyday life, talk is the primary medium for learning, and for that reason, talk is an essential part of learning community life" (1992, 47). However, in the absence of a strong community, students will not be willing to take risks with their thoughts nor offer the ideas that springboard the rigorous construction of meaning.

Engaging in purposeful talk and creating community are reciprocal processes. Each strengthens the other. Peterson notes this very relationship. "In fact, at its best, people are more than partners in dialogue, which has its best chance to flourish when it takes place between people (young and old) who care for one another. This care and trust create a social condition where participants open up and accept not only the other person's ideas, but the person, too" (104). There is something about sitting together in a circle to share ideas and possibilities and working to understand each other's thinking that changes the way we treat people.

Learning communities are not created by generic programs, recitation of oaths and values, special presentations and activities, or other artificial means. Peter Johnston, author of *Choice Words: How Our Language Affects Children's Learning* (2004), shares this same realization. "The most humbling part of observing accomplished teachers is seeing the subtle ways in which they build emotionally and relationally healthy learning communities—intellectual environments that produce not mere technical competence, but caring, secure actively literate human beings" (2). Learning communities result from the day-to-day goings-on when people who respect, trust, and value each other's thinking are challenged with motivating, rigorous learning experiences and offered just the amount of support necessary for success. The authors of *Crucial Conversations: Tools for Talking When Stakes Are High* view these purposeful interactions as vital. Stephen Covey sums their belief up in the foreword, stating that "When you produce something with another person that is truly creative, it's one of the most powerful forms of bonding there is." (Patterson et al., xii).

Also of great importance to health of the community is the confidence and sense of well-being of the individuals inside the community. Peter Johnston speaks of creating a sense of "agency" in children; a belief in their own ability to be successful learners. Children need to believe that, when they take on complex learning in strategic ways, they can be successful. Again, a reciprocal relationship exists: Drawing on the support of the community creates agency, and children with agency create a stronger community.

The idea of a community of learners that supports each other echoes the emerging trend toward combined intelligence in the business world. It sits in sharp contrast to the traditional model of individual learners who bow to an authoritarian teacher. Randy and Katherine Bomer address the importance of the shift toward learning communities. "Only by participating in communities where others are waiting to hear from us, where a group believes our words and thoughts are significant, can we develop a habit of speaking out about things we care about" (2001, 2).

 ## From a Transmission Theory to a Constructivist Theory of Learning

"Ohhh! Teacher! I get it! I know!" Can't you just see the hand waving in the air, the eyes shining, the excited bounce, the other children leaning in to hear words of wisdom? But, what exactly does "getting it" mean? What does it mean to *know*?

The traditional model of education defines "knowing" as remembering and producing a "right answer"; a "right answer" remembered after having been transmitted by the teacher or the textbook.

However, David Perkins asserts that "real learning is a consequence of thinking" (1992, 8). Paulo Freire agrees, arguing for a problem-posing pedagogy that places students in the role of "critical co-investigators with the teacher," and requires them to apply what they know as they think critically about their world (2003, 80–83). Perkins refers to this as "generative knowledge," which he defines as "Knowledge that does not just sit there but functions richly in people's lives to help them understand and deal with the world" (1992, 5).

Constructivism is a theory about how people learn based on this belief that we learn best when we are able to piece together our own understandings rather than passively absorbing information. Children in a constructivist environment understand that they are not being taught to; rather, they take an active role in both the teaching and the learning. This necessitates that the role of teacher becomes vastly different from the image of teacher under the traditional model. In the constructivist model, the keeper, dispenser, and tester of knowledge of old becomes a model, facilitator, and at times, co-learner.

Constructivist classrooms are filled with discussions that allow for negotiation and the construction of understanding, or purposeful talk. When children use talk as a tool for making meaning, each shares his or her thinking through the lens of the child's own understandings of the world. Many different points of view are offered, and as focused talk around these ideas is pursued, all participants emerge with a stronger understanding than what they may have constructed on their own.

An insistence on silence at all times guarantees that children will be forced to think through and make sense of what they are learning in isolation. Yet, all too often, we find traditional classrooms where children are silent, teacher talk dominates, and literal answers formulated by single learners working in isolation are accepted as evidence of comprehension. Or, we find classrooms where the noise and energy level are high, but conversation hovers at the chitchat level; there is little to no evidence of purposeful talk. A transition from silent classrooms to constructivist environments that encourage children to use talk in purposeful ways as a tool for building generative knowledge will enable true "I get it!" moments.

From Right Answers to Valuing Ideas

When I was in school, the "smart" kids were the ones who always had "the answer." I remember that feeling of absolute superiority when I was sure I was the one who had "the answer." My hand would shoot up as I scanned the room to size up the competition. The more hands that waved madly in the air, the straighter and higher mine would push upward, only to flop down in dejection when someone else was picked to proudly proclaim "the answer." The giving of "the answer" meant the exchange was over; there was nothing more to be discussed.

In classrooms where real and complex questions are posed, however, there is not necessarily one answer, or even a right answer. In *Reading to Learn: Lessons from Exemplary Fourth-Grade Classrooms*, Allington and Johnston delve deeper into their research in the classrooms of highly effective teachers, noting that dialogue in these classrooms include large amounts of "tentative talk," which they define as open-ended talk that proposes possibilities and allows others to build off the thinking, complete the ideas, or contribute in other ways

(2002, 205). These classrooms were not geared for answers. Rather, children were sharing and talking about ideas.

I was working with a fifth-grade class at Webster Elementary who were investigating the ways readers tease an author's purpose and point of view from the mix of fact and opinion in a text. We were on our second read of "Let's Rage Against 'Roids," an editorial arguing against the use of steroids, from the fifth-grade set of *Exploring Nonfiction: Reading in the Content Areas*. Our first read of the text was focused on constructing meaning: understanding what steroids were, who was using them, and why. The author's point of view was clear, and the children strongly agreed. Our second read was to determine the author's purpose. Was it simply to inform, or was the author up to more?

The text was on the document camera, and as we read the title, Mikaela's hand shot up.

MARIA: Go ahead, Mikaela.
MIKAELA: (hand goes down, and Mikaela gets confused look on her face) Oh . . . never mind!

These "never mind's" have several meanings. It may mean Mikaela realized her thought didn't connect, that she was moving in the wrong direction, or that she simply forgot. Quite often, though, "never mind" means that a student has an idea that isn't completely clear to them, that they're not sure how to articulate the idea, or that they think the teacher wants an answer, not an idea.

MARIA: No, trust yourself . . . go ahead and say what you are thinking. (That hand shot up for a reason, and that means Mikaela may have the beginnings of a very strong idea.)
MIKAELA: I forgot. ("I forgot" often means "I lost my confidence")
MARIA: It's in there—trust yourself.
MIKAELA: Well . . . (hesitates)—that word, *rage*.
MARIA: What are you thinking about the word *rage*?
MIKAELA: It's, it's a really strong word.
MARIA: Why would the author choose such a strong word?
TRENT: Rage is like really angry. I think the author wants us angry.
DARNEESHA: That's emotion! Authors use it to like get us mad or upset to make us want to do stuff.
CAMERON: So—that's persuasion!
MARIA: Mikaela, so what are you thinking now? (I purposefully directed the thinking back to Mikaela to push her toward completing the meaning that her idea had started us constructing.)
MIKAELA: That author used that word—*rage*—to make us angry . . . like, I think he's angry about steroids, and he wants us angry, too.

ANGEL: He says we should rage—like we'll do it if he says.

MARIA: So, what I'm hearing you say is that the author is using strong language—a strong verb here—to make us feel the way he does?

JOSE: Hey, we need to think about this!

Mikaela was on the right track. There was something to the author's choice of "that word—*rage*." She just wasn't exactly sure what it was. Her ability to share the beginnings of an idea in a community that valued such ideas as springboards for constructive conversations enabled these students to uncover the author's persuasive stance, construct a stronger understanding of the text, and even begin to push back. This purposeful talk would not have taken place in a classroom that valued only "right answers."

For this reason, Jeralyn Treas initiated a series of conversations with her third-graders at Webster around the reasons why children sometimes don't share their thinking. The number one reason her students confessed to was not being sure their answer was right. This propelled the class into discussions about ideas as opposed to answers. Jeralyn assured her children that their work was not about answers, but about growing ideas. "Even if it's just the beginning of an idea," she coaxed, "get it out. Then we can all work to form it, grow it, and learn from it." From that point on, her children participated in purposeful talk more confidently, knowing that their thinking would be supported by others.

These scenarios illustrate the need for teachers to slow down and encourage children to get their thoughts out. Some children are able to clearly articulate ideas, but with others we seemingly need to excavate the thoughts from their heads, and work to find a brilliant idea in the jumble that comes out. But, moving on to the next student, or saying "I'll come back to you," then searching for a "right answer" and never returning, simply lets children off the hook. They don't learn the power that comes from wrestling with an inkling of an idea, shaping and articulating it the best they can, then working with others to enable their idea to gain strength and grow.

 ## From Testing to Talking as Assessment

The American education system is staggering under a forced obsession with tests. Norm-referenced, criterion-referenced, standards-based, pretest, post-test, practice test, test ready, test fatigue. In our quest to leave no thing untested and no one behind, it seems at times that what we've left behind is our common sense.

Bruce Marlowe and Marilyn Page, authors of *Creating and Sustaining the Constructivist Classroom* (1998), question the purpose and end result of excessive testing. "As such, traditional testing formats may be good measures of what students remember; rarely, however, are they good measures of what students can do or of what they understand" (62). While it is important to determine the degree to which an individual child has achieved goals set by standards, it is far more crucial that we assess their proximity to these goals and their development of intelligent behavior, identify needs and/or obstacles that may be standing in the way, and plan an effective instructional course.

Often, simply taking the time to listen and talk with a child (or eavesdrop on their talk with others) can be the greatest information-gathering opportunity possible. Listening to children talk gives us a window into their thinking. As we listen, we gain an understanding of how actively they are constructing meaning, the level of complexity they are able to reach on their own and through purposeful talk with others, and the strategies they may be using to do so. We are able to determine not just the memorization of facts, or chance hits on right answers, but whether children are actually constructing new knowledge using "the norms of good reasoning," as called for in New Standards.

However, absence of specific ways of thinking in children's talk, or even the absence of talk itself, does not necessarily equate with a lack of ability. To gain access to the full range of children's thinking, we must move beyond listening, and actively engage children in conversation.

While some assessing of an individual's thinking naturally occurs during whole class and small group interactions, the opportunity to pull up close to a child or partnership offers an opportunity for more in-depth conversation and specific exploration of a child's current level of understanding and strategy use. Conferring is a means of doing just this. Conferring with readers is not about firing off questions from a predetermined "hit list." As we confer with children to assess reading, we note what they choose to discuss and the language they use to describe their interactions with the text. As we talk, we are determining what each child can do and what his or her next steps might be.

At times, a progression of increasingly supportive questions may be used to assess children's level of independence with thinking about text in ways that are absent from their conversation. For example, I was working with a group of fourth-graders who had studied character motive in realistic fiction. The children were now reading historical fiction and biography. In addition to gathering the range of information that presents itself during conferences, the classroom teacher and I wanted to assess whether thinking about character motive was transferring across genres to determine our progression of minilessons. We sat down next to two girls, who were reading *Amelia and Eleanor Go for a Ride: Based on a True Story*, by Pam Muñoz Ryan (1999). Our questioning to determine their thinking about character motive is shown in Table 3–1.

While a test would have simply shown that the girls did not know what motivated these women—at least not yet—through conversation we now know that the girls had done quite a bit of work thinking about the interplay between characters and setting, and what was in these women's hearts. They simply needed a nudge to take the next step.

Listening to children's talk gives us a sense of what children can do, which enables us to plan next instructional steps that build on the known. Note that the questions in Table 3–1 could have continued to narrow to the point where an either/or (50/50) question could have been asked. *Do you think Amelia and/or Eleanor were motivated by this or that?* If the children are able to make and support a choice with evidence, then you know there is some degree of understanding and ability to think in a particular way.

Question	Intention Behind Question	Children's Response
What are you thinking?	Discover whether child or partnership is thinking about character motive independently.	Talk was about the excitement of flying and how cool it was that these two women were friends.
What are you thinking about these two women?	Focus the child's thinking and talking more specifically on the characters.	*She's (Amelia) the pilot. Women didn't really do that then.* (Talked more about the women's flight together and how courageous they were.)
Yeah, that would be courageous. I'm wondering, if this was all so unusual for women back then, what do you think made them do these things?	Further focus the thinking and talking on character motive specifically.	*Hmm . . . well, we think (looks at partner) . . . maybe it's 'cuz, well, they were brave.* *Well, yeah and—but—oh! You mean like character motive!? We didn't really talk about that.* *Maybe . . . we gotta reread!*

Table 3–1

Equally valuable information about children's thinking can be gleaned from listening to their questions. In classrooms where only the teachers ask questions, the children are not able to constructively ask for support at their point of confusion or informational need. When children ask questions, they are telling us exactly where their thinking has paused, how aware they are of their own confusion, and what they are attending to. In this sense, assessments gained from listening to children's talk are not used to determine children's limits or failures, but to inform and design instruction.

When we take the time to reflect on these five powerful beliefs and conditions that have permeated classroom life for so long, and consider the evolution of thought around each, we take the first steps toward making the shifts that will support our efforts to enable purposeful talk. As the purposeful talk grows and we—teachers and children alike—experience its power, the talk itself becomes the driving force behind the transformational process of leaving educational practices and beliefs of the past behind us and working toward enabling our children to meet the challenges of the world that awaits them.

Getting Started

Environments and Instruction that Enable Purposeful Talk

The way human beings learn has nothing to do with being kept quiet.
—Ralph Peterson

To achieve our goal of strong purposeful talk, we must create an environment that will allow conversational behavior to develop, and teach children the norms of that behavior.

Classroom Environments that Invite Thinking and Talking

If you watch any of the currently in-vogue home remodeling or total home makeover programming, you will hear designers talking at length about creating spaces that are both functional and socially inviting. Kitchens are not designed solely with cooking in mind; rather, they are a gathering place for socializing while cooking. Living-room design is not just about choosing the couch, the coffee table, and side seating; once they are chosen, they are arranged again with conversation in mind.

Our classrooms need to be thought through with an understanding that learning has a strong social component, and space that invites conversation must be part of their design, as well. Even when empty, our classrooms speak volumes about our pedagogical belief system and values. A quick peek through a window can tell the experienced eye whether the children or the teacher take the dominant role in thinking and talking in this space.

A physical environment that allows for purposeful talk can be created through a mix of furniture and space. Tables where children cluster, ample carpet space with room for all, and cozy corners for partners and small groups announce that thinking and talking together is valued here. Desks in rows, individual seats, and no space large enough to accommodate everyone say something completely different.

Of primary importance in classrooms that enable purposeful talk is a large carpeted area where children are able to meet to engage in the construction of meaning, problem solving, inquiry, and other conversations. The carpet must be roomy enough for the children to sit in a circle, as this arrangement allows all to face each other. Facing each other strengthens communication by allowing for eye contact and nonverbal communication, and allows us to weigh the reactions of others to our ideas. Margaret Wheatley, author of *Turning to One Another*, quotes a colleague when discussing the importance of the circle: "Human beings have always sat in circles and councils to do their best thinking, and to develop strong and trusting relationships" (2002, 9).

The classroom library should also encourage collaborative endeavors. Library shelves can be arranged to create sections or pockets that house different genres. Then, children have space to settle in as they browse or research and discuss the books themselves, or their topic of interest. Kid-size furniture adds an element of coziness, and invites small group or partner conversation.

Round tables, as opposed to individual desks, offer a gathering place where all come on equal terms. There is no head of the table, no one person elevated above the others. While my children always had their own seat as a "home base," they moved around freely during the day, partnering or grouping at different tables as they engaged in various academic endeavors.

Classroom wall space needs to be considered as a crucial piece of the learning environment, created to be both visually inviting and academically supportive. Walls that strengthen efforts at purposeful talk would include a variety of charts. Charts with tracks of thinking and talk from current and past units of study, charts that trace the process of building conversations, conversational phrases that support the pursuit of ideas in depth, and charts that support partnership talk are just a few of the possibilities. Charting will be explored in depth in Chapter 7.

Arrangement of the charts on walls needs to be strategic, with charts that support specific types of talk visible from the places children tend to gather for these conversations. Charting that no longer needs to be on the walls can be hung on clip hangers on a clothes rack in the back of the room. This allows for continued access on an as-needed basis.

 ## Teaching Conversational Behavior

Once the classroom is arranged in ways that support conversation, we are ready to begin teaching children to engage in purposeful talk. Most of our learners come to us knowing how to chitchat, share ideas with a friend while they play, tell about things, and give us reports on how they are feeling. But, the heightened level of engagement necessary for purposeful talk may be something new to them. They will need support in getting started.

Hearing All Voices

To construct the strongest meaning possible, we must make sure we are hearing the voices of all of our children. As with any group of people, adults included, some children will dominate the talk, while others manage to create a corner to hide in—even when seated in a circle. Helping children to become aware of who is talking, and how often, helps. This is not for the purpose of praising those who talk and criticizing those who don't; rather, it is a time to discuss the role everyone must play, and allow children a chance to reflect on their pattern of participation.

Learning that purposeful talk necessitates turn taking, and learning how to both take and give those turns, can be difficult. Some children negotiate entry into conversations easily. Others need support in gaining entry. Some simply need time to linger on the author's or their peers' words and think before talking. English language learners may need time to translate their thinking. Once those who speak out easily understand that others need time to think and formulate (or translate) their first reactions, they will work on holding off, and checking with others before speaking.

Likewise, speakers sometimes need a moment to pause and think while speaking, and should be allowed to do so without others jumping in. Teaching children to wait a few seconds or even ask the speaker if he or she is finished can avoid interruptions and the feeling of being bulldozed by a more loquacious speaker.

Allowing children to rehearse and strengthen their thinking through a turn-and-talk with a partner before sharing whole group can give the less-confident children the support necessary for joining a whole class conversation. It also gives our English language learners support in translating their ideas. And, most importantly, it requires all children to talk, even if it is just with one other person.

At key points during a Read Aloud or Shared Reading, or any time I begin to hear a buzz about the text, I may ask children to turn and talk. This means turning to the person sitting next to them in the circle to initiate a conversation around their thinking. The turn-and-talk time is not "I'll tell you my idea, you tell me yours . . . OK, we're done!" Rather, it is the same level of listening and purposeful talk we use in whole group. Turn-and-talk time allows children a chance to test their ideas, gain input and grow them stronger, or change their minds and move their thoughts in a new direction.

During the turn-and-talk, we listen in to the children's conversation to assess understanding. If the next step is to be whole group conversation, I listen for a pair with strong ideas developing and have them kick off the whole group talk by sharing their thinking to that point.

Some children do not participate in conversation because they have difficulty staying "tuned in." Helping children to focus their listening through the lens of a question or a particular way of thinking can help them to listen with intent and develop a thought to share.

Kenny was a second-grader whose mind tended to wander during Read Aloud and the ensuing conversations. Giving Kenny a question to hold on to before we read added an extra level of support.

"Kenny," I would lean over and say before starting to read, "we're going to read the first few pages, then I'm going to ask you what you think about this character. So, listen and think, and have an idea ready to start us off. Here we go . . ."

As I read, when something important happened with the character, I would give Kenny a knowing look, as if to say, "This is huge! I can't wait to hear your thoughts!" By the time I finally stopped reading and turned to him, Kenny would be bursting with ideas to share, and more apt to listen to others and engage in the talk that sprang from his thinking. As Kenny developed the realization that listening with intent enabled this, his listening began to improve. And, as his listening improved, his level of participation greatly increased.

Growing Ideas

Once we have our learners focused and all members participating in the talk, we need to begin building conversations that truly move our construction of meaning to new levels. Allowing children to simply share their own thinking without any accountability to each other's thinking or a purpose will not enable this.

Saying Something Meaningful ◆ A first step in developing purposeful talk is to be sure children's thinking is grounded in the text or their understanding of the world through the text, and pushes the group's construction of meaning. Our youngest learners often share thoughts that pop into their heads by playing word association games. They hear something in the text, which makes them think of something else, and off they go!

How familiar does this sound, primary teachers? You are reading aloud a fabulous text, such as *Chester's Way* by Kevin Henkes. You've just read the part about Chester's breakfast, which is always the same: toast with jam and peanut butter. Suddenly, a voice leaps out from the circle. "I like jam with my peanut butter. Strawberry's the best. Once, my mom . . ."

And, you know that if you let this sharing continue, soon every child in the circle will be weighing in with their favorite jam flavor and jam story. Yes, this is thinking and talking, but is it purposeful talk that will help us to build bigger understandings about Chester, the classic control freak? The stronger conversation would be about why Chester is this way, and how this affects those around him.

If we have cultivated a caring and respectful environment in our classroom, we can say to our young jam enthusiast, "Wow, I like jam, too. But I'm wondering if thinking about jam right now is going to help us to understand Chester? Sometimes things pop into our head as readers, and we realize that it's taking our thinking away from the text, rather than pushing us deeper into the text. When that happens, we park our idea on the side of our brain, and refocus on the story."

When we are consistent, this careful refocusing and reminding children of our purpose with our talk will gradually eliminate random comments that hijack conversations. As our children grow stronger with sharing meaningful thoughts, we then need to be certain that children are actually listening to each other. Purposeful talk cannot occur without the same degree of effort at listening.

Listening with Intent ◆ "Hearing is a sound; listening is a thought." This insightful distinction comes from Michael Optiz and Matthew D. Zbaracki's book *Listen Hear! 25 Effective Listening Comprehension Strategies* (2004, 2). We hear sound constantly. Most of it, we ignore. Our brain filters it out. Unfortunately, this filtering out seems to occur as we try to build purposeful talk in the classroom, too. We need to teach children that listening with intent, or listening with active attention to meaning, is at the heart of purposeful talk.

Listening with intent involves letting the idea being heard into our brain, and actually engaging with it. One reason children don't listen to each other in this way is that they are too focused on remembering their own idea. As adults, we do the same thing. We form, rehearse, and strengthen our own thinking as we wait our turn to share it, and do so with such deliberateness that, while we may hear others speaking, we don't truly listen to their message.

To listen with intent, children must learn that, once someone starts talking, their hands go down; they temporarily "park" their thinking, and focus on the idea being shared. Most certainly, some children will forget their thought as they listen, but the process of learning to listen with intent is far more valuable than one idea about one text. And, over time, the children do become stronger at holding on to their own thinking while simultaneously listening to others and engaging with the others' thoughts.

Preoccupation with their own thinking is not the only reason children do not listen to each other, however. All too often, I am invited into classrooms to help teachers uncover the reasons why talk does not seem to be flowing between the children. When classroom talk is scripted to show the conversational dynamics in the classroom, the obstacle becomes visible. Frequently, children don't listen or talk to each other because they don't have to! The problem is that the teacher is repeating everything each child says, and in a clearer, more concise manner. Why would any member of the learning community listen with intent to a peer, putting in the effort to understand their thinking, if the teacher is going to repeat and clarify? A smart learner would wait for the teacher! This is not to say that we should never clarify children's thinking; it just can't happen all the time. Otherwise, we end up with talk moving between the teacher and one individual child, and everyone else waiting their turn to speak to the teacher. These children never have to listen critically, use talk purposefully, or say things like "I don't get you!". There is no negotiating of meaning together, just a dependence on an adult whose high level of support prevents the very thing that she is trying to develop from happening at all.

To truly want to listen to each other, children must also value each other intellectually. Pointing out individual students' contributions helps to build an identity of intelligence. So, when we say, "Addie, when you put those two ideas together for us, it helped us to understand that . . . ," others become aware that Addie has the capacity to think in smart ways. You can bet the next time Addie joins in on the talk, others will listen!

Along with this valuing of each other's thinking, there needs to be an understanding that a constructive process allows for ideas that are bigger and better than any one individual is able to formulate on his or her own. In Chapter 3, we discussed the debriefing of process as a step toward developing reflective intelligence. As we debrief process, we help children to see that their talk was truly a collaborative, constructive process. Making this process visible creates a sense of urgency about listening with intent.

Keeping Lines of Thinking Alive ◆ Once children are listening with intent, we up the ante, expecting that the children will not only listen, but stay focused on that single idea, work to understand the thinking behind it, and develop the idea as far as possible.

So, when Miriam shares her thoughts, we cannot allow Samuel to say, "Well, I think . . . ," and go off in a different direction. We have to say, "Hold on—what do you think about Miriam's idea?" By doing this, we are asking for connected thoughts that will keep a line of thinking alive, pushing it as far as possible.

Phrases that support the pursuit of an idea in depth have been proposed for helping children with the language and conversational moves of purposeful talk. Charts such as the one in Table 4–1 are becoming standard in classrooms

Purposeful Talk
• I agree with you . . . • I disagree with you . . . • I can add on . . . • I have evidence . . .

Table 4–1

where purposeful talk is valued. Unfortunately, these language stems are often used as an end rather than as a means of developing stronger thinking.

Let's think about these three uses of the "I agree" phrase from the chart.

Conversation A:
Two first-grade children are reading *The Snowy Day*, by Ezra Jack Keats.

MIGUEL: I think the snow melted.
TATIANNA: I agree with you. It melted.

Here, the "I agree with you" phrase was used to say the same thing. There was no purposeful constructing of stronger meaning.

Conversation B:
Two third-grade children are talking about *At the Edge of the Forest*, by Jonathan London.

BRANDON: *His heart raced* . . . I think he's scared for the coyote. He thinks it might die.
SHAQUELIA: I agree.

In this situation, the "I agree" phrase was used to say nothing. It excused the user from thinking!

Conversation C:
Two sixth-grade children are reading the poem "Rabbit" from *Baseball, Snakes, and Summer Squash*, by Donald Graves.

ABRAHAM: I don't think his ears are probably that bad. Bullies just do that to you. They make you think something is bad or matters when it's nothing.
LAKESHA: I agree, and they did make up—they built the hut!

While both ideas were strong, the "I agree" phrase was just thrown out to give the second child entry. She then changed the line of thought, keeping the two from exploring the first idea in depth.

All of these children are meeting the demands of the talk chart in their classroom, which is simply to use the phrases. But, is this purposeful talk aimed at negotiating meaning?

If we capture the children's natural language during their own conversations, and help them to understand the way the phrases they naturally use construct meaning, we can circumvent the need for the artificial use of language scaffolds. The scaffolds can still be part of the chart for those who need them;

others are free to make the same discourse move in their own way. This charting may look like the chart in Table 4–2.

The chart in Table 4–3 takes this support a step further. While the language on the chart in Table 4–2 is truncated, the entirety of a thought as expressed during whole class conversation is captured on the chart in Table 4–3. These thoughts with a recording of the context can then be used as benchmarks, with the specific language we want children to take note of, the role it played, and its result underlined for emphasis.

Supporting children in learning the role that language plays in making conversational moves that develop ideas, and making that language visible, helps to strengthen purposeful talk.

Natural language	What you are doing as a listener/ thinker/talker	Why learners do this when talking purposefully
• "Oh, yeah …" • "That's what I thought, and …" • "Me too, because …" • "That's just like …" • "I agree with you because …"	Agreeing	• To support an idea • To cite more evidence • To make the idea bigger and stronger
• "No, no, …" • "Wait, but …" • "I don't think …" • "But …" • "I disagree with you because …"	Disagreeing	• To offer a different opinion • To clarify something the speaker misunderstood or did not hear
• "Yeah, and …" • "Oh, and then …" • "That's because …" • "And also …" • "I can add on …"	Adding on to an idea	• To support an idea • To cite more evidence • To make the idea bigger and stronger • To give explanation or example
• "I don't get you!" • "Could you say that again?" • "Could you say more about that?" • "What do you mean?" • "Why?"	Clarifying meaning	• To clarify something the speaker misunderstood or did not hear • To clear up confusion

Table 4–2

Natural language	What you are doing as a listener/thinker/talker	Why learners do this when talking purposefully
Marissa said, "The author is quoting an expert." Then Julio said, "Yeah, that could mean the author is trying to persuade us."	Julio was adding on to Marissa's idea.	This made Marissa's idea bigger and stronger because it added importance to what she noticed. Now we really get why we should notice what authors are doing.

Table 4–3

 ## Negotiating Meaning

As children learn to stick to ideas and develop them in depth, they will begin to vocalize stronger opinions about the ideas and push back and forth at each other's thinking. Now, the true negotiation of meaning begins! We need to make sure this process involves positive exchanges that strengthen understanding rather than becoming all-out arguments.

When keeping a line of thinking alive and negotiating meaning, total agreement is neither necessary nor always possible. What children do need to learn is a healthy respect for differences of opinion when the other point of view has strong evidence, and a willingness to consider alternative views even if they are not swayed in the end. Listening to ideas that are different from ours helps us to look at situations with new eyes.

To be flexible with thinking, children must first listen with the intent of understanding the reasoning and evidence behind differing ideas by allowing them to develop through talk. Then, they need to consider the plausibility of the different interpretation, and weigh it against their own.

Issy, one of my second-grade students, was a model of flexibility, and always took this process to heart. Listen in to this piece of a conversation about Eleanor Roosevelt that Issy had with Desiree, a third-grade student, while reading the afterword of *Eleanor* by Barbara Cooney. The girls are discussing Eleanor's visits to an orphanage with her father, and the impact it had on her life.

DESIREE: I think she helped the poor people because she cared. She learned because of her father. He was smart to take her to those places with the poor people, the boys, so she could see.

ISSY: But that's mean. He shouldn't take Eleanor there. She was little—look! (flips to picture)

DESIREE: Yeah, but he was teaching her. See, it says *Eleanor soon found out* . . . Her dad wanted her to find out about the poor people.

ISSY: No, but Desiree, she had to work and stuff. Dads, they don't, they shouldn't make their kids do that! Why would he do that?

DESIREE: Because, look how she was (flips back another page). She's all fancy— like the dress, the mom's dress, and the house, they had Nanny . . .

ISSY: Oh—and the necklace!

DESIREE: Yeah, she didn't know about the boys because she didn't live like them, so she had to find out.

ISSY: Oh, so she could care?

DESIREE: Uh-huh—see (flips back to the afterword) it says *all her life*. Her dad started it and she never stopped.

ISSY: Oh! Ooohhh . . . Now I'm disagreeing with myself. I think it wasn't mean . . .

Desiree's idea did not sit well with Issy initially. Instead of discrediting the thought, she engages with Desiree, asking her to explain her thinking. Issy listens to the evidence, asks questions, admits confusion as the idea develops to push Desiree for more, and in the end, is willing to change her mind.

Remember, the objective is not "winning" as in a debate, but constructing meaning. What's most important is that children learn to listen to the ideas of others, value their thinking, be flexible and willing to let go of ideas in the face of compelling evidence to the contrary, and be interested in understanding other points of view even if, in the end, they are not swayed.

 ## Let's Listen In

So, what might instruction that teaches purposeful talk sound like? Let's listen in to a few minutes of a conversation in Maricela Cruz's first/second-grade Sheltered Immersion classroom at Garfield Elementary in the San Diego Unified School District.

On this day, Maricela was using a Mondo product, *Let's Talk About It*, which is a collection of amazing photographs intended to initiate small group talk for the purpose of oral language development. Maricela was taking the liberty of using a *Let's Talk About It!* photograph rather than a text to initiate and teach a beginning lesson on the process of developing purposeful talk. The photograph was of a school bus on a deserted mountain road. A mother bear and two cubs were crossing the road behind the bus.

MARICELA: Let's take some time to just think, what might be happening here? (Waits a few moments, models a thoughtful stance . . . "Hmmm" . . . face scrunches up a little.) This is how thinkers look when they're thinking! (Many students imitate her expression, and gaze at the picture.) Let's turn and talk. Build a conversation with your partner about your thinking. (Students turn immediately to predetermined partner and begin to talk.)

ANTONIO: (in partnership with Kelvin) The bus is on a road at the mountains. I think the bus driver went too far. He ran out of gas.

KELVIN: Yeah, he went to the mountains . . . it's not the school. How will he get the gas? They're stuck. I think . . . why did he?

ANTONIO: Why did he go?

KELVIN: Yeah.

ANTONIO: I think he got lost.

KELVIN: Whoa—that's really lost!

MARICELA: Let's come back together. I'm going to ask Carmella to share what she and her partner were thinking. Listen to their idea and see what you think.

CARMELLA: I think the bears are crossing the road to get food.

MARICELA: Hmmm. (Looks around the circle expectantly.)

ERIC: Yeah—they cross the road to get to the trees to eat.

JUAN: I have a different idea.

MARICELA: Could you please hold on to your idea? Let's stick with Carmella's idea and see how we can build it bigger.

SASHA: I can add on.

MARICELA: Oh, so Eric has added that the food is in the trees, and you have something else that can grow Carmella's idea?

SASHA: I think there's a lake in the trees. They're going to the lake to eat fish.

MARICELA: So you took Carmella's idea of crossing the road to get food, and Eric's thought about food in the trees, and grew it even more by adding your thinking about there being a lake and fish. (Looks around the circle expectantly again.) What do you all think?

FERNANDO: Well . . . but, I think bears, they like honey.

SASHA: They like honey and fish!

We can see the tracks of Maricela's work with her children in this little snippet. This group of children is at the beginning phases of learning to have purposeful conversations and negotiate meaning. Maricela facilitated their effort by allowing children think time and the opportunity to try out their ideas in a partnership first. She then orchestrated the talk to pursue lines of thought, reminding children that their job is always to build bigger ideas, and expected that all were listening and thinking for this purpose.

Let's rethink the construction of the conversation. To start, Maricela gave her children think time, modeling for them what this looks like and sounds like (quiet). She could have supported further by using a Think Aloud, however, a Think Aloud gives a predetermined direction to the conversation, and Maricela did not want or need to take that heavy of a hand.

From there, she moved into rehearsal time with a partner. Many children need time to translate their thoughts into English, or find the right vocabulary and structures to communicate with clarity. And, many are unsure of expressing ideas in large groups, as this way of thinking and talking together is new to them. The rehearsal time with a partner allows children a chance to get ready and build confidence by trying out their idea in a partnership first. Note Maricela's explicit wording. "Build a conversation with your partner" conveys a very different message than does " Tell your partner what you are thinking." Tell is a one-way experience; building a conversation implies give-and-take of thought that grows.

Both Antonio and Kelvin (as well as others in the class) immediately turned to each other in what Ardith Davis Cole refers to as the "knee to knee, eye to eye" position (2003). They listened to each other and stuck with the same idea, growing it by adding details and questioning each other.

Maricela listens in to partnerships for assessment purposes, and then calls the group back together to build a larger conversation. She starts this by having them listen to the ideas formed by one set of partners. This was a very strategic move. First of all, this partnership was on a train of thought that Maricela knew the others could build on. Second, Carmella is very shy. Maricela wanted her to share her idea while it was fresh from partnership rehearsal and gain confidence by experiencing other children growing their thinking.

Notice that Kelvin, and later on, Eric, use the everyday phrase "Yeah" rather than "I agree with you." This is the way they naturally speak. Maricela does not demand that they desert their natural language for scaffolds, as the end result is a natural flow of purposeful talk. Sasha, on the other hand, gains entry to the conversation using the "I can add on" scaffold.

After Carmella shares, Maricela does not edit, approve, or disapprove, and does not fill in the moment of silence with her own talk. Most important, she does not repeat the idea. There is an expectation that all learners take responsibility for listening to Carmella.

Kelvin and Antonio realized that their thinking did not immediately fit with Carmella's idea and held on to it. When Juan tried to shift the talk to an unrelated idea, Maricela gently asked if the new idea could be saved so that the class might pursue the current line of thought. This is crucial. Often, out of kindness and concerns over self-esteem, we allow the group to be taken off topic by children who raise their hand or join in with random or different ideas than the one being discussed. But, if we are teaching the power of purposeful talk, we cannot allow this. Other ideas can be saved without hurting feelings. Maricela did return to Juan and have him share his idea once Carmella's idea had been discussed, and the class talked it through as well.

When Sasha offered to bring the conversation back on track, Maricela defined what adding on would do. After Sasha added her thoughts, Maricela articulated for the children the way Carmella's, Eric's, and Sasha's ideas fit together to form something bigger, essentially tracking the progression of thought for those who needed support in following the conversation. Maricela then turned to the others and asked for their thoughts on what had built to that point.

Fernando disagreed with Sasha, and used his natural language to do so. Sasha listened, and then made use of Fernando's disagreement to strengthen her own thinking. All of this happened without Maricela saying a word!

Throughout this process, Maricela orchestrated without dominating. Her thoughtful, expectant pauses reminded the children of their role and responsibilities. She did not get nervous about silent moments or fill them with her own chatter. Maricela waited for the children, and let them know through eye contact that she not only expected more, but knew that more was coming. She understood that this was cognitively demanding work, and that time to think is crucial to the process of building purposeful talk and negotiating meaning. What might talk in our classrooms sound like if all of our children learned to converse this way?

Growing Purposeful Talk
Using Read Alouds as the Spark

Reading and writing float on a sea of talk.
—James Britton

Jesse Harrison and her third-graders were on their third read of *The Summer My Father Was Ten* (1999), by Pat Brisson. In this beautiful picture book, a daughter retells the story of her father's tenth summer, and the way a thoughtless act of destruction while playing baseball near his neighbor's garden led to a friendship that transcended time. Jesse and her children had paused in their reading as the father stood, looking at the now empty lot where his neighbor, Mr. Bellavista, used to plant his tomatoes, peppers, and onions.

JESSE: (reading from text) . . . *but he just couldn't make the words come out.*
BENJAMIN: (purposely seated next to the teacher to support engagement) He looks at the empty lot and he can't forget because he knows it shouldn't be empty.

DAMON: Yeah, he can't get it out of his mind. It's so sad.

JESSE: Oh, why so sad?

DAMON: It's because a garden should be there, but they wrecked it, and the other sad part is when you want to say 'sorry' but you can't, it's, like, like it said, his body won't go.

ANDRE: It's like your brain knows, it's trying, but your body can't.

KEYSHA: In his heart I think he feels like he needs to say 'sorry.' His heart is pumping really hard, and he feels very nervous.

DIANA: Yeah, I felt that before. Just like it said, the words, they won't—it's too hard to say them.

KEYSHA: Sometimes I can't say 'sorry' because I don't know why I did something, so I'm nervous and scared. But I feel bad.

SHANTE: Yeah, that's how he is—the father—he knows how they shouldn't have wrecked the garden, and doesn't know why they all did it. He knows what he has to do, but it's hard. He feels bad. But he has courage to follow his heart.

DIANA: It's like we can do that, too.

Through their talk, the children constructed critical insight into the father as a person, the change he goes through, and ultimately, the heart of the story. And, they were on the verge on taking that next step: using their understanding of the heart of the story to affect the way they live in the world.

The level of complexity in the children's talk was not a chance happening. It is the product of thoughtful planning, explicit instruction, modeling, and orchestration of purposeful talk in the highly supportive instructional approach of Read Aloud. This chapter addresses text choices and lesson design that supports children in thinking and talking to negotiate and construct meaning, and enables teachers to orchestrate the talk, all in the context of Read Aloud.

 ## Read Aloud: The *to* on the *to*, *with*, and *by* Continuum

Pearson and Gallagher's Release of Responsibility Model (1983) offers us a framework for considering instructional approaches and support structures that enable the transfer of ways of thinking and talking about reading to independent practice. Figure 5–1 offers an adaptation of this model with an added foundation of a belief in talk. Only within a community that allows talk to thrive will children develop the habits of mind that bring purpose to their talk.

During Read Aloud, the most supportive instructional approach, we are teaching children to think about text in increasingly complex ways. Simulta-

Release of Responsibility Model with instructional approaches and supports that move children towards independence.

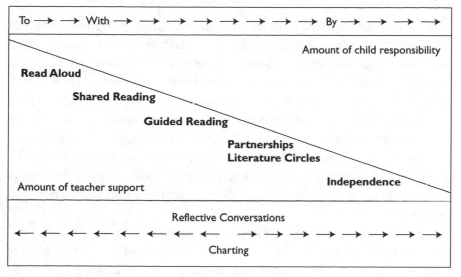

Figure 5–1 Release of Responsibility Model

neously, this is the time to teach children what purposeful talk that constructs deeper meaning sounds like, how it works, and how valuable it is. Taking responsibility for the reading enables us to use complex text that the children may not be able to access on their own. We support the construction of meaning with thoughtful lesson design that scaffolds children's thinking, allows us to preplan modeling and questioning, encourages purposeful talk, and enables orchestration of that talk.

As we orchestrate talk around rich text, children begin to engage in the negotiation of meaning that is the hallmark of purposeful talk and constructivist learning. Ralph Peterson reminds us that, "Through negotiation, students come to understand how someone else interprets an event, text, or situation; thereby, the basis for their own understanding is broadened" (1992, 81). The negotiation during Read Aloud, supported by the teacher, creates for the teacher an assessment opportunity to determine the children's next steps in conversational behavior, and offers the children their first steps in the creation of a habit of mind crucial for becoming purposefully literate: an expectation that there will be other perspectives, and a desire to listen to and understand them for the purpose of enriching our own thinking.

◈ Text Selection

Strong conversations in the Read Aloud begin with smart, thoughtful text selection. Compelling text is a must for engaging students in thinking and talking about their thinking. Fiction texts that compel children to have purposeful and powerful conversations that construct stronger understandings and build habits of mind are generally realistic, have characters with an appropriate level of depth that the children care about, and deal with universal issues and feelings that enable the children to connect and apply their thinking to real life. The text does not necessarily need to be about a familiar place or topic. After all, one purpose of being literate is that reading helps us to experience new places and situations. In essence, it is the heart of the text, not the setting or situation, that must matter, or "hit home."

A perfect example of a text whose topic is unfamiliar but whose heart "hits home" is Eve Bunting's *Train to Somewhere* (2000). In this story, set late in the 1800s, a group of children from an orphanage in New York are sent West by train for adoption. Many teachers shy from this text, feeling that most children cannot connect to a story about the despair of the orphanages of long ago or a journey with a purpose such as this. However, we must differentiate the literal text from the heart of the story. *Train to Somewhere* dances around universal themes such as hope, fear, and possibility. Children can connect to and understand these ideas. An understanding of the characters' plight will develop during the Read Aloud as the children build purposeful talk.

It's important to note that, especially with books intended for primary children, characters don't need to be human to be realistic. First-graders fall in love with the Poppleton series by Cynthia Rylant year after year. They have no problem connecting deeply with and caring about a talking pig that lives next door to his best friend, a sometimes annoying but always dependable llama. The characters in Kevin Henkes' books are equally as real to children. What child has never felt jealousy like Lilly, suffered with teasing like Chrysanthemum, or worried like Wemberly? And who among us did not wipe away a tear when E. B. White's Wilbur gave Charlotte that last good-bye wink?

Using nonfiction text for Read Aloud can present unique challenges. Dense factual text, when read aloud, often overwhelms children. To be engaging as a Read Aloud and compel children to think and talk purposefully, narrative or lyrical nonfiction texts about topics that interest children may be a better choice. Selected excerpts of informational text can certainly be read aloud as well, but

nonfiction text with beautiful color photographs, captions, and other supporting features, including visual, organizational, or graphic aids, may be better
choices for Shared Reading because they provide children visual access to all
sources of information as they construct meaning.

 ## Thoughtful Planning

Before we begin planning for a Read Aloud that utilizes purposeful talk as a tool
for negotiating and constructing meaning, we must invest the time to read the
text and know it well ourselves. We must have a sense of the rich meaning we
hope the children will build. With fiction text, this means not only knowing the
literal story, but developing our own understanding of the heart of the story (big
idea, or theme). Complex text may encompass more than one theme, so flexibility and an awareness of the options is crucial. Then, we must plan ways of
supporting the children in drawing on the heart of the story as they consider
their own interactions with the real world.

Of course, the children's ability to negotiate and construct meaning at the
deepest levels a text offers will depend on their experiences and immersion in
units of study that teach ways of thinking about text (explored in Chapter 6).
But, to create a vision of possibility, we are going to explore conversation
around texts at the richest level of meaning, assuming an instructional background that enables these conversations.

To illustrate this, let's first consider a fiction text, "The Pudding Like a Night
on the Sea" from *The Stories Julian Tells*, by Ann Cameron (1989). The literal
story is about Julian, his little brother, Huey, and his dad, who are making pudding for Mom's birthday. When the pudding is done, Dad naps, and the boys
find themselves unable to resist the pudding's lure. Unplanned conversation at
the literal level with this text usually builds around pudding: the process, the
ingredients, the messiness, and favorite flavors, in addition to how much the
boys ate, how much trouble they'll be in, and the essential question, "Why don't
they just get the kind in the cups at the grocery store like my mom does?"

But, if all the children talk about is pudding, or the literal, how will their talk
ever build toward the heart of the story? And, if they don't build a strong sense
of the heart of the story, how will they lean on the literary experience as they
navigate life in the real world?

Planning for talk that builds toward the heart of the story begins by envisioning just how this talk might sound. We begin with the end—or talk indicative of

strong comprehension—in mind, then plan backward as we consider how we will draw this level of purposeful talk out of the children. The heart of "The Pudding Like a Night on the Sea" dances around Julian and Huey's relationship with their father, so talk needs to build around this, not pudding.

To draw out talk that builds toward the heart of the story, we must determine the essential stopping places in the text. These stopping places may include spots in the text that allow the reader to construct an understanding of the characters and the interactions between characters; gain a sense of setting if it plays a crucial role; and focus on change and the causes of the change, among other things. There is no right or wrong when deciding on the exact places to stop, as long as you are able to draw talk from the children that builds purposefully toward the heart of the story.

Table 5–1 shows possible stopping places for "The Pudding Like a Night on the Sea."

Next, we need to have a sense of what talk that is indicative of strong comprehension should sound like at each stopping place. Then, we plan questions for these stopping places to encourage this talk. When planning our questions, we need start with open-ended questions that offer the children an opportunity to think strategically, share their thinking, and do the work for themselves before supporting the effort with more specific questions. Often, we give children too much information by embedding what we hope to hear in the question.

If we are trying to build a sense of the father, a pivotal figure in understanding the heart of the story, what we don't want to do is start the conversation by asking, "Why is this dad such a good dad?" Instead, we begin with a general question, such as, "What are you thinking?" This question allows us to gain an overall sense of the children's thinking and gauge where they may be needing support in constructing meaning.

Then, if all we hear is literal talk about making pudding, we might decide to focus the conversation on the characters by asking a more deliberate question. Table 5–2 shows a progression of increasingly more supportive questions that might be asked if a general "What are you thinking?" does not do the trick.

These more supportive questions, along with other scaffolds, need to be planned to keep the talking and thinking focused throughout the Read Aloud if necessary, and lift the conversation beyond the literal if that is all we hear. As we plan for each of the stopping places in the text, we must consider: How will I craft a more supportive question in case I need one? Is there a place in the text I might reread as a support? Can I support the children in using prior

Stopping place	Reason for stopping
After the description of the dad	To develop a sense of what Dad is like.
Partway through the pudding making	To gain a sense of how hard it was to make the pudding.
When Dad tells the boys to leave the pudding alone	Too good a prediction spot to skip!
As the boys are eating more and more of the pudding	Hold this up to what we know about Dad— how will he react?
When Dad discovers the pudding is almost gone	Gain a sense of how Dad feels and why. Predict using what we know about Dad.
When Ann Cameron is playing with the words *beating* and *whipping*	Compare what children *think* is going to happen to what we know about Dad, his relationship with the boys, and the way a dad should react.
Once children make sense of *beating* and *whipping*	Make sense of this based on what we know about Dad, strengthen our understanding of their relationship and what kind of father he is.
At the end	To think about the lesson the boys learned, how they changed, how having this kind of father helped, and how this helps us to think about parents in the real world and their relationships with their children.

Table 5–1

knowledge or making connections? How might I model my own thinking if necessary?

Of course, we must always be prepared for the possibility that our children will take the talk in an absolutely brilliant direction that we failed to consider. When this happens, we listen with intent and join in on the construction of meaning!

Stopping during the Read Aloud, asking questions and building talk that constructs an evolving meaning as the reading progresses, not only supports an

Comprehension goal	Possible questions from Least supportive → → → → Most supportive		
Developing an understanding of the father	What are you thinking about Dad and Julian and Huey?	What kind of father do you think Dad is?	What does the fact that Dad takes time to make pudding with the boys for Mom tell you about him?

Table 5–2

understanding of the text, but is the first step in teaching children a habit of mind that will enable them to think and talk in this way on their own.

Returning to "The Pudding Like a Night on the Sea," let's consider the evolving meaning we hope to construct, and the increasingly supportive questions that might be used to scaffold the process if necessary. Table 5–3 offers one possible progression of thinking, talking, and questioning.

Finally, to push the children's thinking and talk toward the heart of the story and beyond, we need to use our understanding of the characters and change; in this case, the lesson the boys learned and the way it will affect their future behavior. We might ask a general question such as, "What do you think Ann Cameron really wants us to think about?" Or, a slightly more supportive question such as, "We've been discussing the boys and the way they learn from their dad. Why would Ann Cameron write a story that gets us thinking and talking about this?" Or, an even more supportive question: "What does this tell us about families and how they live and grow together?" The important thing is not so much the exact phrasing of the question, but its ability to push the children to use their previous conversation to generalize and talk about deeper issues in the text, issues that we all deal with in the real world. Shifting the thinking in this way enables readers to use well-written text to help them live smartly in the world. We'll talk more about this in Chapter 6.

Thoughtful planning for a Read Aloud of nonfiction text requires supporting children in moving beyond the literal, or the collection of facts, toward bigger ideas in the text, an understanding of the author's purpose and point of view, and their own thoughts on the topic. It's not that we don't want children to marvel at facts. To the contrary, nonfiction readers should not only *ohh* and *ahhh* over cool information, but must linger over it and work to make sense of it. To

Stopping place	Reason for stopping	What talk indicative of meaning-making might sound like	Possible scaffolds if the children aren't constructing strong meaning
After the description of the dad	To develop a sense of what Dad is like.	He is a unique character, lively and smart. He can be really happy, but when he's mad, watch out! (Maybe difference in opinion of whether this makes a good father—that's OK!)	• What are you thinking? • What is Dad like? • Does he sound like a good father? May need to reread and model think using the description of father.
Partway through the pudding making	To gain a sense of how hard it was to make the pudding.	Wow—they're working hard. Everyone has to help, and it's a big mess to clean up.	• What are you thinking? • What do they have to go through to make this pudding? • Does it sound like a lot of work? • Why didn't they just buy pudding that's all done?
When Dad tells the boys to leave the pudding alone	Too good a prediction spot to skip.	Oh no! They're going to sneak some! I know I would . . . they'll get in trouble! If I did that, my mom/dad would . . .	• What are you thinking? • How does it feel to be tempted by something? • What do we know about these boys, and boys in general? What do you think they'll do?
As the boys are eating more and more of the pudding	Hold this up to what we know about Dad—how will he react?	They won't stop—they're going to eat it all! Dad worked really hard, and he'll find out, and when he gets mac . . . But, he sounds like a nice dad. Disagreement here is OK, as long as ideas can be backed with evidence.	• What are you thinking? • How would a dad react to this? • What do we know about *this* dad? • What do you think he'll do? • Why?

continued

Table 5–3

Stopping place	Reason for stopping	What talk indicative of meaning-making might sound like	Possible scaffolds if the children aren't constructing strong meaning
When Dad discovers the pudding is almost gone	• Gain a sense of how Dad feels and why • Predict using what we know about Dad	Oh boy—he's mad now. All his hard work, and it was for Mom. Remember what the book said about Dad when he's mad?	• What are you thinking? • How would you feel if someone ate something you worked hard to make for someone else? • What about Mom's birthday? • Reread description of Dad again. Think aloud to help children understand how that information might help our thinking.
When Ann Cameron is playing with the words *beating* and *whipping*	Compare what children *think* is going to happen to what we know about Dad and his relationship with the boys, and the way a dad should react.	Oh no! They're going to get spanked. Hey, I didn't think he was that kind of a dad!	• What are you thinking? • What do you think Dad means by *beating* and *whipping*? • Does this match what we thought we knew about Dad?
Once children make sense of *beating* and *whipping*	Make sense of this based on what we know about Dad, strengthen our understanding of their relationship and what kind of father he is.	Oh, that's what he meant. He was just scaring them—maybe to teach them a lesson. That's kind of mean, but next time they'll remember—so maybe it's OK. He must love them, because he really was mad, but he handled it in a smart way.	• What are you thinking? • What did Dad mean when he said *beating* and *whipping*? • Why would he scare the boys like that? • What does it tell you about him as a dad? • Does this make sense with what we thought we knew about Dad?
At the end	To think about the lesson the boys learned, how they changed, how having this kind of father helped, and how this helps them to think about parents in general and their relationships with their children.	Now they don't want to get near the pudding! They learned a good lesson. They will never be that thoughtless again—this is a big change. Dad was smart to have them discover how hard the pudding is to make. Parents should be smart like that and teach a lesson instead of yelling and punishing.	• What are you thinking? • Why didn't the boys want any pudding? • Do you think they'll do something thoughtless like this again? • What does this tell you about Dad? • Do real dads behave this way? Should they?

Table 5–3 *continued*

ensure strong thinking and talking, we want our children to hold new information up against what they think they know, ask questions, form theories, read for evidence, and consider how the information links together and leads them toward bigger ideas.

Because we negotiate some forms of nonfiction differently than we do fiction, our planning may be different. Just as with fiction, we plan our nonfiction Read Aloud backward. That is, we start by envisioning what strong talk that moves beyond factual information alone (the literal) might sound like. But, before we plan stopping places, we plan for the way we will move through the text. Will the entire text be read aloud, or just selected sections? If reading just selected sections, which sections, and why? We must select the sections purposefully, then plan the stopping places that will allow purposeful talk to build.

To illustrate this, we'll use the picture book *Watching Desert Wildlife*, by Jim Arnosky. *Watching Desert Wildlife* (2002) is a collection of short nonfiction passages written in first-person narrative, which highlights the diversity and amazing adaptive characteristics of desert wildlife. This text is not only compelling enough to be read aloud in its entirety, but its sections are complete enough to stand on their own as a Read Aloud that models the thoughtful navigation of nonfiction text based on purpose. Any of the passages might be used for Shared Reading as well, which creates many instructional options.

One possible plan for a Read Aloud of *Watching Desert Wildlife* for the purpose of determining the big idea, author's purpose, and point of view is charted in Table 5–4.

When we read aloud only portions of a nonfiction text like this, the children often ask to take the text off to partnership and independent reading so they can continue their thinking. As each reader or partnership reads, they leave tracks of their thinking with sticky notes, and then pass the book along. This keeps the thinking growing, and encourages transfer of thinking about text in specific ways to independent practice.

A lesson planning template that has proven helpful in designing Read Alouds with this attention to deeper meaning, progression of questioning, and orchestration of purposeful talk can be found in Figure 5–2. The Read Alouds of "The Pudding Like a Night on the Sea" and *Watching Desert Wildlife* were designed to support children in negotiating a very complex meaning. To be successful in thinking and talking through text in these ways, children need experience with a progression of thinking and talking curriculum that builds in complexity. Chapter 6 will address these curriculum needs.

Stopping place	Reason for stopping	What talk indicative of meaning-making might sound like	How to scaffold if the children aren't constructing strong meaning
Front and back cover and quick glance through Table of Contents and several pages	• Briefly activate schema • Orient readers to the text	Oh—the desert. I've been there/seen pictures. It's really cool. It says "wildlife"—that's probably plants and animals. This book might have some of the plants and animals I saw. Hmm … there's an Introduction. That usually tells us more about the book.	• What are you thinking? • What do you know about the desert that might help get you ready to read? • How should we go about reading this book based on our purpose?
Introduction	• Continue text orientation • Form theory around a possible big idea, author's purpose, and point of view • Gain a sense of the author	So, he really wanted to see the desert because it's so different. This book has lots of different animals, so maybe it's really about the animals that were the most different, the coolest ones he saw. He seems to really be amazed by them.	• What are you thinking? • What have we learned about our author? • What did Jim Arnosky notice about the desert? • Why might he have written this? • What big idea is he wanting to share with us?
Section about desert birds in general	• Be amazed by cool facts • Flexibility with schema • Understand more about author's point of view and purpose • Read for evidence to support theory about big idea, or abandon/change mind	He does seem amazed because of the way he describes the birds. The wren holds on to spines with its toes! I thought that would hurt them—that nothing could get close to a cactus. I think he wants us to be amazed, too. He said the desert is different from where he lives. Maybe he wants us to know that different places have different animals, and they survive there in smart ways.	• What are you thinking? • What does Jim Arnosky think about desert birds? • Do you agree? • How are desert birds like and not like the birds where he lives? • Why would he point this out?

Table 5–4

Stopping place	Reason for stopping	What talk indicative of meaning-making might sound like	How to scaffold if the children aren't constructing strong meaning
Section about the Gila Monster	• Be amazed by cool facts • Flexibility with schema • Make sense of information • Understand more about author's point of view and purpose • Gather evidence to support theory about big idea or abandon/ change mind	Did you hear how they bite? I thought lizards were just no big deal. I didn't know some could hurt you. I think they're nocturnal—it said they're most active at dusk. Maybe that's because it's so hot. Or, maybe that's when their food comes out, when it's cooler. I's the way they survive the heat. Jim Arnosky is amazed by this, too! And, I think he wants us to be amazed. So, maybe that is the big idea of this book. I think the book is really about how these animals survive in smart ways.	• What are you thinking? • What amazed you? • How does Jim Arnosky feel about this animal? • Why is he writing about this? • Does this information fit with our theory about the big idea?
Section on Elf Owl	• Select portions of the text to read based on purpose and theory of big idea • Be amazed by cool facts • Flexibility with schema • Make sense of information • Gather evidence to support theory or abandon/change mind	Wow, I didn't know an owl could be that small. It lives in a cactus. Maybe that's because there aren't any trees. So, the desert animals do find smart and unique ways to survive. That is the big idea. It's lucky the woodpeckers are there to make the holes. The animals actually help each other. I think desert animals are pretty cool, too!	• What are you thinking? • How are you feeling about desert animals? • Does this information fit with our theory about the big idea? • What do we think Jim Arnosky's purpose and point of view is? • What do you expect from the sections we didn't read based on our theory?

Table 5–4 *continued*

Planning for Purposeful Talk and the Construction of Meaning

Title _____   Date _____

Deeper meaning in text: *Big ideas, theme, and/or critical understanding children should construct (either in this read, or over several reads).*	Instructional Focus: *Way of thinking and talking about reading children are studying.*	
Text: *Phrase to cue you for stopping places based on focus point and to allow for the construction of meaning.*	Questions, wondering, or comments: *Open ended means of getting the thinking and talking started.*	What talk should sound like: *A sense of what you might hear at this point in the construction of meaning.*	Scaffolds to support the thinking and talking if necessary: *More supportive questions, places in text that might need rereading, model thinking, etc.*

Closing: *close the conversation by recapping the meaning constructed, and debriefing the process.*

Reflection: *thoughts about children's use of talk to construct meaning, progression with the focus, unexpected confusions or struggles, and implications for next instructional steps.*

Figure 5–2

◈ Orchestrating the Talk

As the children's talk begins to reflect stronger thinking as a result of thoughtful planning, we must consider how to keep the conversations focused for the constructive work of negotiating and building meaning. In their book *Questioning the Author* (1997), Isabel Beck, Margaret G. McKeown, Rebecca L. Hamilton, and Linda Kucan identify six Discussion Moves teachers use for just this purpose. They are:

- marking: responding to specific ideas in a way that highlights them
- turning back: holding children accountable for their thinking and the text
- revoicing: interpreting what a child is attempting to express, and rephrasing it so others are able to think alongside and build off the idea
- modeling: making our thought process visible for children
- annotating: filling in information that children are not able to construct from the text or have no schema for
- recapping: summarizing ideas that have been constructed up to a particular point in the conversation

The following snippet of conversation is part of a larger conversation my second- and third-graders and I were constructing from another Julian and Huey story, "My Very Strange Teeth," from *The Stories Julian Tells*, by Ann Cameron.

In this lively story, Julian has an old baby tooth and a new tooth in the same space in his mouth. He doesn't want to wait for the old tooth to fall out, so Dad suggests various barbaric methods of extracting the old tooth (using pliers, or tying a string from the tooth to a doorknob). Julian wisely decides that maybe having two teeth in one space isn't so bad after all.

During the piece of the conversation charted in Table 5–5, four of Beck's Discussion Moves were used to support purposeful talk and the construction of meaning.

Recapping, Revoicing, Turning Back, and Marking helped to purposefully orchestrate this conversation toward deeper understandings of Julian's feelings, Dad's motives, and the eventual understanding of the heart of the piece. Annotating and Modeling were not used in this snippet of talk. Julian's tooth dilemma was familiar territory for most children, so annotating was not necessary. Modeling was equally unnecessary, as the children were able to think and talk through the deeper issues without higher levels of support.

Classroom Conversation	Beck's Discussion Moves
MARIA: So, what are you thinking? CHENELLE: He wants his tooth to come out. KENNY: Yeah, his tooth is loose, and he doesn't want to wait like two weeks, and he doesn't want two teeth there, the one that is growing in and the old one that is growing out. TAMARA: It could be even longer—like months! That's TOO long to wait! JAILYN: Well yeah, because like I agree with you, because you know how people get embarrassed and stuff. That's embarrassing—it's why he says 'I can't wait!' MARIA: So, you're saying that he wants the old tooth out because he's embarrassed by it, and he's getting impatient? CHILDREN: Yeah! MARIA: Reads the parts where Dad offers to use the pliers or tie a string from the tooth to the doorknob. ANTHONY: I would be scared. MARIA: Say more about that. ANTHONY: With all the stuff Dad said, he might be, well, not scared, but like umm . . . ISSY: Afraid? ANTHONY: Yeah, afraid it might hurt. Dad might hurt him. JAILYN: Well, I agree with you, because like, you know, if he wants to make the teeth come out then you know how people just like, how people make it, like you know how Issy just loose her tooth and even her Dad didn't like pulled it and stuff, or do that, tie it on the door. MARIA: So, you're saying that Julian's dad is suggesting things that your dads wouldn't do? JAILYN: Well, yeah. MARIA: Let's think about what we know about Julian's dad. Does it make sense that the dad would want to hurt him? TROY: He's tricking him! You know in the other stories, he tricked him to do all the work. But he won't trick him. Julian's gonna wait. MARIA: Oh! Troy's saying Dad is **tricking** Julian. JAILYN: Like, I agree with you, Troy, because you know how parents just trick children about getting your tooth out. Like, 'you won't feel a thing.'	**Recapping:** By summing up the previous comments, the talk was bundled in a way that allows the conversation to move on. Recapping can also be used to retrace the meaning that has been built to a particular point when conversation stalls. This gives everyone a chance to rethink, and those who didn't follow the talk the first time have the opportunity to catch up. **Revoicing:** Restating a confusing or complex thought allows others access to the ideas. Jailyn, an English language learner, needed support in making her idea comprehensible to the others. **Turning Back:** Encouraging children to reexamine their thinking leads to deeper thinking. Beck also uses this term to describe moves that teachers make to hold children more accountable to the text. Encouraging the children to hold their thinking up to what they knew about the dad enabled a new idea to emerge. **Marking:** The highlighting of an idea as important by emphasizing it in some way. Troy was using what he knows about the dad from the other Julian stories we had read. I used my voice to emphasize, or mark this idea as important, and encourage more conversation.

Table 5–5

◈ Using the Turn-and-Talk

At times during a Read Aloud, we stop and immediately build the conversation as a whole class, as was done in the talk excerpts from *The Summer My Father Was Ten*, and "My Very Strange Teeth." Building conversation with the whole class works well when a variety of voices are contributing, the pace is lively, all are listening with intent, and the negotiation and construction of meaning is purposeful.

There are times, though, when we offer children a chance to prepare for the whole class conversation by turning from the circle to a partner and talking with the partner first. During these turn-and-talks, children have an opportunity to process, try out, and strengthen their thinking with their peers, then come together and use their partner talk to build a whole group conversation, which the teacher then orchestrates. A turn-and-talk can be preplanned. Any time you suspect that students may need time to process a response to a complex part of the text, you can ask them to turn and talk first, mine the partner talk for "gems" to begin the whole class conversation, then come together to build that whole class conversation.

A turn-and-talk can also be spontaneous, used when too many voices are silent. A turn-and-talk requires all to get their thinking out, as children have an immediate responsibility to their partner. While children are talking with their partners, the teacher is able to listen in and gauge their level of comprehension. If the quiet is due to confusion, listening in to the partner talk will help to pinpoint the confusion, and allow the teacher to support the children in backing up and constructing meaning.

The turn-and-talk is equally valuable any time many voices are clamoring to be heard all at once. These spontaneous explosions of meaning usually happen at major "ah-ha" spots in a text, natural prediction points, or events or feelings children readily connect with.

Midway into that third read of *The Summer My Father Was Ten*, Jesse's students had one of those explosions.

JESSE (the teacher): (reading from text) *. . . but still, Mr. Bellavista made no move to plant.*
DARCIE: Probably Mr. Bellavista hasn't started to plant because he's scared to.
JASMINE: Oh! I was thinking the same thing! Mr. Bellavista thinks that if he plants again, the boys will go in and play and ruin the garden again.

MANY VOICES: Oh! Oh, yeah! (Hands shooting up) That's what I think too . . .
   yeah, you had my same idea . . . it has to be because in the picture . . .
JESSE: OK, OK, turn and talk—what makes you think this is what Mr. Bellavista
   is thinking?

This "ah-ha" about Mr. Bellavista seemed to electrify the group. Jesse realized
that many children were eager to give voice to their reasoning for thinking this
way, and a turn-and-talk gave each child an opportunity to be heard.

Whenever children turn and talk, I am out of my seat, listening in on conversations. Table 5–6 highlights the importance of the turn-and-talk both for
children and teachers.

After a brief minute or two of turn-and-talk time, the children are called
back together to begin building a larger conversation. I begin by asking a partnership that was off to a strong start to share their thinking. "Let's come back
together. Anthony, you and Marla were talking about why this character was
behaving in this way. Would you share your thinking, to get us started?"

If I'm aware of conversation in another partnership that adds to or builds on
this idea, I will direct the conversation to them right away. I might say something like, "Vanessa and Manny, your talk about the characters' feelings goes
right along with this. Will you add on and keep the talk going?"

If I'm not aware of another conversation that builds, I will open up the
opportunity to build by asking, "Who can add to that idea, or work with it in
some other way?" Or, "What do the rest of you think about this idea?" We'll
consider new ideas with input from all voices until they seem to reach their full-

The turn-and-talk gives children an opportunity to:	The turn-and-talk gives the teacher an opportunity to assess:
• Process their thinking out loud • Rehearse their idea with partner feedback • Strengthen their idea through partner input • Change their idea based on ideas and/or evidence they had not considered • Clarify areas of confusion • Translate their thinking into English or access vocabulary with partner support	• Level of individual comprehension • Strategies children are using • Holes in children's understanding . . . and to mine small conversations for big ideas that will serve as a springboard for whole class conversation

Table 5–6

est potential. Then, I recap the talk, quickly summing up our understanding to that point, and move on.

As Table 5–7 illustrates, transitioning from the turn-and-talk to whole group conversation and working to keep a line of thinking alive teaches children to listen with intent and build off other children's thinking. And, it allows us continued opportunities to assess, orchestrate, nudge, and teach content along with the value of talk.

This process can take place at each major stopping point during the read. Or, you can use a mix of talking and constructing meaning in whole group with the turn-and-talk used at particular points in the text that warrant its extra support or the need for all to talk.

Moving from the turn-and-talk to whole class conversation gives children an opportunity to:	Moving from the turn-and-talk to whole class conversation gives the teacher an opportunity to:
• Compare and contrast their thinking with other's thinking • Practice articulating a co-constructed idea or point of view with clarity, drawing on their partner to support them • Practice supporting a co-constructed idea or point of view with evidence from the text or knowledge of the world, drawing on their partner to support them • Learn the importance of listening with intent • Grow their thinking stronger by listening to others' ideas • Follow a thought as it grows • Practice flexible thinking • Practice ways of disagreeing that are positive and respectful • View purposeful talk as positive and energizing • View purposeful talk as a means of negotiating, understanding, and rectifying differences • Develop habits of mind	• Assess partnerships and the class as a whole in general • Assess a child's amount of participation in partnership versus whole class • Orchestrate the talk toward deeper understandings using the bits of partner talk that were listened in on • Nudge children toward strategic thinking • Teach for transfer

Table 5–7

For partner talk to flow efficiently without unnecessary pauses in the thinking and talking, students should know in advance who they will turn and talk with. Long-term partners are best, as you will not need to reestablish who talks to who every Read Aloud. Partners simply come to the circle next to each other. When one is absent, they turn to the closest partnership and join in.

In Susie Althof's kindergarten class at Webster Elementary, students routinely practice their turn-and-talk before the reading begins. "Show me how you're going to turn and talk to your partner," Susie prompts. Immediately, children turn knee to knee, eye to eye, as Ardith Davis Cole (2003) describes. Many of Susie's children sit with elbows on their knees, chins in their hands, gazing at each other with smiles. Some reach out and hold hands, others lean in to each other. These children clearly love this! "Show me you're ready to learn together again" Susie calls out. Just as quickly, all turn their attention back to Susie, ready to engage in a great read.

In Stephanie Hasselbrink's fifth-grade class, partners come to the circle together, sitting close enough that just leaning over enables them to begin a turn-and-talk. To be sure, the cute knee to knee, eye to eye, adoring glances are gone, but not the richness of the talk. Because these same partners talk during every Read Aloud, and are also partners as a support for independent reading (to be discussed in Chapter 7), these children have a history of past conversations and other shared text to draw on as they work to construct meaning with the current Read Aloud.

Careful text selection, thoughtful planning, tools for orchestrating talk, and partner support are crucial ingredients for teaching children to think and talk for the purpose of negotiating and constructing rich meaning. They are the scaffolding pieces that offer children that "Hey, I can do this!" feeling. Supporting children in their thinking and talking about text is not enough, however, if they are not taught ways of thinking and talking that enable them to construct the deepest meaning possible. Our next step is to consider the content of our instruction. Chapter 6 will explore Units of Study as a means of offering children a continuum of increasingly complex ways to think and talk about their reading.

Thinking and Talking About Reading in Increasingly Complex Ways

Immersing Children in Units of Study

Education is not the filling of a pail, but the lighting of a fire.
—W. B. Yeats

As our lesson design becomes stronger and our ability to orchestrate talk builds, we must also add to the mix instruction that increases children's ability to think and talk about their reading in increasingly complex ways. For this purpose, we design units of study that immerse children in these new ways of thinking and talking. Children may progress through as many as six to eight studies in any given year. The decisions we make about the content and flow of studies during the year are a balancing act between children's assessed needs, deep comprehension of grade-level text, state and national standards, and children's progress toward or beyond both of these.

As we design studies, we must be mindful that our endless pursuit of literate lives for ourselves and our children is not just about understanding text. Rather, our constructed understandings are a vehicle for imagining possibilities; we become literate for the purpose of crafting a more just world and living in it in smarter ways. Alan Luke and Peter Freebody have proposed four families of practice, or roles, that readers need to lead such purposefully literate lives (1990). These roles are:

- ◆ Code breaker: How do I crack the code of this text?
- ◆ Text participant: What does this text mean?
- ◆ Text user: What do I do with this text here and now?
- ◆ Text analyst: What does this text do to me?

Of the four roles, those of text user and text analyst, which require the reader to take a critical stance, are often the most challenging . . . for us, not the children! Most of us simply never learned to question and push back at text critically. Yet, it is only when we use rich meaning of text to open conversations about the ways of our world and our role in perpetuating or challenging these ways that we are becoming purposefully literate.

Our work in this chapter will focus on teaching children to think and talk as text participants, text users, and text analysts. The roles are not hierarchical, with text analyst being saved for later years. Likewise, our conversations about a text should not necessarily be a linear progression from text-based comprehension to thinking and talking beyond the text. Children's talk may dance from text-based to beyond the text and back to text-based as they think and talk their way through a read.

We will look at overviews of instruction in fiction and nonfiction and draw studies from these overviews, as well as a study that supports children in reading, thinking, and talking purposefully between genres. The overviews are not intended to be the entirety of our work with children in these genres; rather, they are a range of possibility to support study design.

Getting at the Heart of a Story and Using It to Live Smartly in the World: Reading, Thinking, and Talking About Fiction

Authors Randy and Katherine Bomer ask, "How can we extend the imagination it takes to live inside a book—the ability to make meaning and build the world of the story—to a social imagination, a belief that we can make lives better and more just for people?" (2001, 55). As we move from talk grounded in text to talk that drives toward the heart of the story, we are developing an understanding of the ways of our world. Purposeful talk about these ways allows children to consider their own response to their world, and envision grander possibilities; to co-create social imagination. Yet, even with the conversational support of others, getting at the heart of a story is complex work. To reach this goal, readers must understand the interplay between story elements and how this interplay leads to conflict, resolution of the conflict, and change.

The chart in Table 6–1 is an overview of instruction that supports children in learning to think and talk about text in ways that help them tease out the heart of a story and move beyond. Aspects of this work begin in kindergarten, and continue each year with more complex text and more in-depth study. A sampling of the type of questions that push children as text users and text analysts runs the length of the chart as a reminder that children's thinking and talk should move between text-based and beyond the text. Although the chart lies on paper in a linear format, our work with fiction is cyclical.

From this overview of instruction, we are then able to zoom in on focus points and design studies appropriate for children based on needs and grade-level standards. In kindergarten or first grade, a study lasting approximately four to six weeks might focus entirely on understanding characters. Table 6–2 is one possible crafting of a character study. When planning studies, I always include an expectation for children's talk. Once children are thinking about their reading in this way, what should their talk sound like? This is an extension of the backward planning discussed in Chapter 5.

Primary classrooms might progress from a study of character to studies that intertwine the story elements. Even kindergarteners are quite capable of thinking and talking about themes in text and should be encouraged in that direction.

In our upper-grade classrooms, work with story elements would need to have a greater degree of complexity. Assuming children have some foundation in the interplay between story elements, the work would begin with some review using more challenging text, and move quickly toward and focus on understanding and using the heart of the story. Table 6–3 illustrates a possible progression of an upper-grade study.

As you immerse children in this work, consider selecting a core of perhaps five complex texts to work from. Picture books are a wise selection at all grade levels, as the length allows children to have many experiences thinking and talking about story elements in intertwined ways to make meaning in complete texts, beginning to end. Use of picture books, as mentioned in Chapter 2, also

		Thinking as a text user and text analyst
Focus point	**How readers do this**	
Understanding the character(s) *Fiction readers need to understand their characters deeply.*	We get to know our characters through: • What they do • What they say • What they think • What other characters say or think about them • How other characters behave around them • What the narrator reveals about them We need to understand: • Character complexity • Character motive • Character interaction	Why did the author write this? Who should read this? Why are the characters portrayed in these ways?
Paying attention to the role of setting *Fiction readers need to understand the place and time in which the story takes place.*	We need to consider: • Whether the setting plays an active, crucial role, or is just background • What significance there may be in the era the story is set in (the way the world at the time affects the characters and events) • How the setting affects the characters' thoughts and behaviors	Are people really like this? Who has the power in this text?
Following the plot *As events unfold, fiction readers consider how the story moves through time, and what events seem most significant.*	As we think through the events over time, we tease out: • Events that cause the characters to think and behave in different ways • Effects those events have on setting (i.e., a war ruins a beautiful village)	Is this a fair representation of our world? Should it be this way?

Understanding change
 	
Fiction readers need to recognize change and understand its causes.
	We pay special attention to:
	
	• Character change as caused by
	  - interaction with other character(s)
	  - setting
	  - events (e.g., war, natural catastrophe)
	• Setting change as caused by
	  - character
	  - events
	• Changes in events (e.g., war ending) as caused by
	  - characters
		What is our role in perpetuating or changing this?

Using change to understand the heart of the story and beyond *Fiction readers uncover real-world issues in texts and use them to think smartly about the world.*	We ask: • What is this text really about? • What aspect of our world did the author want us to think about? • Why is this important?	

Overview of instruction that enables readers to think and talk about fiction texts as meaning-makers, text users, and text analysts.

Table 6–1

How do readers get to know characters deeply? How does this help them to really understand the story?			
Focus point	**How readers do this**	**What the talk might sound like**	**Being a text user and text analyst**
Getting to know what's in a character's heart *Fiction readers need to understand the character's thoughts and feelings.*	• Use what the character does, says, and thinks to form a theory about a character. • Read on. • Track evidence, be willing to form new theory if evidence doesn't support.	*I think this character is really ___ because he did/said . . .* *Yeah, now I'm sure the character is ___ because here in this next part, he said ___. He shouldn't say that!*	Is this character believable? Did the character behave in a way that people really behave?
Noticing changes in the character *Fiction readers notice when a character behaves in an unusual way and work to determine whether this is temporary, surprising behavior, or real change.*	• Compare what the character does, says, or thinks to previous ways. • Read on to find out if this new way continues (real change), or if the character goes back to his or her usual behavior (surprise).	*Hey, wait! Now, he's acting like he's ___. He wasn't like that before. I wonder why . . .* *Yeah, he's doing it again. He must be really ___ now.*	Why did the author craft the characters in this way? Would you behave this way?
Understanding what caused a character to change *Fiction readers consider all influences on a character as they work to understand why the character changed.*	• Use what the character does, says, and thinks. • Think about the way the character interacts with other characters. • Think about the effect of the setting and events on the character.	*When ___ happened, it seemed to make him ___.* *This other character made him ___.* *I think he's acting that way now because ___.*	What does the author seem to want his/her readers to really think about? Why? What do you think?

Table 6–2

supports our English Language Learners. The Appendix offers possibilities for compelling text choices from which a core of text may be selected for this work.

The third-grade teachers at Webster Elementary worked through the study in Table 6–3 with a thoughtfully selected core of picture books, including many of the titles in the Appendix. For the first two reads through the texts, they focused on the interplay between story elements, designing lessons that pushed

	How do readers understand change in a fiction story? How does this help them to understand the heart of a story? How do they think about the heart of the story in ways that help them to live smartly and/or create change in our world?		
Focus point	**How readers do this**	**What the talk might sound like**	**Being a text user and text analyst**
Understanding the interplay between story elements and their effect on each other *Fiction readers use the interplay between elements to notice and understand the cause of change.*	• Consider characters' effect on each other, if any. • Consider the setting's effect on the character and vice versa, if any. • Consider the event's effect on the character and vice versa, if any. • Be alert for change • Use the interplay between elements to explain the change	*When ___ was happening, the character was . . .* *But now, when ___ changed, the character began to . . .* *He seems to be acting that way all the time now . . .* *I think it's because . . .*	Why did the author write this? How does he/she see the world? Does everybody think this way about our world? Whose point of view is missing? Who should read this? Who has the power in this text? Is this a fair representation of our world? Should it be this way?
Using change to get at the heart of the story *Fiction readers use thoughts and conversation about the cause of change to help them consider bigger ideas about the text.*	• Think about the reason for change, and how this compares to the real world. • Use this to consider the author's message about our world, and our own thoughts about this aspect of our world. • Compare this to other authors who write about this same aspect of our world.	*It all happened because . . .* *That really happens in the world. Once, I . . .* *I think the author wants us to think about . . .*	
Using the heart of the story to think about our world *Fiction readers use the bigger ideas in the text to rethink their world.*	• Does our world really work in this way? Should it? What is our role in this? How can this change? Should it? What can we do?	*It's not right that this happens . . .* *I always . . ., but now I think . . .*	

Table 6–3

children to think and talk about the characters in increasingly complex ways, then upped the ante by asking the children to consider the role of the setting and its effect on the character, and important events and their effects on the characters and setting. Finally, they reread the texts a third time, with lessons designed to orchestrate the talk toward the heart of the story and beyond.

By the third read of each of the texts, we found three things happening:

◆ Struggling students, who tended to be more literal in their thinking, were having the kind of "ah-ha's!" that strong students tended to have on the first or second read.

◆ Other children were able to pull out subtleties and deeper issues in texts and construct understandings well beyond what was possible in the first reads, including thoughts about the crafting of the texts.

◆ English Language Learners were participating more confidently in the talk, using some language from the text and phrases they had heard other students using as conversation built over the course of each read.

Let's listen in to this portion of another conversation from Jesse Harrison's third-grade classroom. This time, Jesse and her children were on their third read of *An Angel for Solomon Singer* by Cynthia Rylant. This is a poignant story of a man, alone in the world, who finds friendship and a sense of belonging in the middle of New York City. At this point in the Read Aloud, the class was considering how understanding character change supports thinking about the heart of a story, and how they can use the heart of a story to live smartly in the world. They were even starting to question what many consider an unfortunate but accepted reality of our world.

KIARRA: Sometimes when people leave their home, sometimes they, um, miss their home and wish for what they're used to. He's (Solomon Singer) used to Indiana. But now he doesn't really have a home, and that's sad.

KEYSHA: When you're at home, you have friends, and you have confidence. Everything's what you're used to.

RAMIKA: But at the men's hotel, there's probably no one there that likes him, nobody in there that takes care of him. That's why he's going to the West-Way Café.

EDWARD: Now, he has friends and confidence. People need it to feel at home.

DIANNA: Yeah, that's true because I was scared here at first when I was new here, but now it feels like home.

JESSE: So, this is something that happens in the real world. Do you think that's what this story is really about?

KEYSHA: It's about how we can make people feel at home, like Angel did. He's like a lesson for us. But I think it's what we should do.

JESSE: Can we take this on right here at Webster?

KIARRA: Whenever we know someone's new or doesn't feel at home, we can welcome them.

These children had dug deep into what Solomon Singer was missing in his life, and were on the verge of pulling out one possible theme. They were questioning realities of our world and their ability to change this reality.

As adults, we know how crucial rereading complex text is for constructing this level of meaning. Yet, selling children on rereading text can be very difficult. The difficulty may be caused by the rarity with which we actually model the purposeful rereading of text for children, and allow them to experience, through careful planning and talk, deeper levels of comprehension as a result of the rereading. Generally, we select a new Read Aloud each day, plow through it, set the book aside, and select a new Read Aloud for the next day. No wonder our children do the same thing in their own reading!

It's Real, But Is It True?: Reading, Thinking, and Talking About Nonfiction

Thinking and talking about nonfiction text as a text participant, text user, and text analyst requires children to read with active, questioning, perhaps even suspicious minds. As we design nonfiction instruction, we must think broadly about text choice. A steady diet of informational forms of nonfiction, where texts are simply a dump truck of facts, not only creates a narrow definition of nonfiction, but gives children a false sense that nonfiction is always true. To avoid this, we use a variety of text, looking purposefully for pieces with bias and opinion, and create studies that teach children to construct meaning by slowing down, thinking about and reacting to the material they are plowing through. To be critically literate, children must determine the author's point of view, question his or her purpose, and hold this up to what they know of the world. The possible progression of focus points in Table 6–4 may be used to develop a variety of studies at many different grade levels. Again, it is not intended to represent the entirety of work within the nonfiction genre, nor should it be considered as a necessarily linear progression of instruction. A sampling of the types of questions that push children to think as text users and text analysts is also included, as before.

Again, an overview such as this allows us to zoom in on focus points and design studies appropriate for children based on needs and grade-level standards. First-graders may need to study the way readers allow themselves to stop, be amazed by, and make sense of the information they are reading. Table 6–5 illustrates one way such a four- to five-week study of active, engaged nonfiction reading appropriate for emergent and early readers may be designed.

	Overview of instruction that enables readers to think and talk about nonfiction texts as meaning makers, text users, and text analysts.	
Focus point	**How readers do this**	**Thinking as a text user and text analyst**
Reading with a wide-awake mind *Nonfiction readers pause in their reading, and say "wow!"*	• Notice amazing information • Pause and think	
Making sense of information *Nonfiction readers take the time to process information so that it's understandable.*	• Compare and contrast information • Connect new information to known information • Think actively about the information	
Asking questions and forming theories *Nonfiction readers wonder and question as they read and work actively to gain the information that will satisfy their curiosity.*	• Allow ourselves to wonder • Form theories • Read on to affirm or discard theories • Form new theories if necessary	
Reading between the information in the features and running text *Nonfiction readers integrate information from running text, photographs, captions, diagrams and other features.*	• Scan the text for a sense of what is included prior to reading • Study and make sense of photographs, captions, charts, diagrams, etc. • As you read running text, pause and refer back to other sources of related information	Do I agree with this author? Is this a valid argument? Is this the way the world should work? How can I take a stand or take action on this information or issue?
Using schema flexibly *Nonfiction readers need to be alert for information that is different from what they thought they knew, and adjust their thinking or question the information.*	Ask yourself: • Does this fit with what I thought I knew? • Why is this different? Consider: • Publication date • Author's expertise • Other sources if not convinced Be willing to change mind if evidence is compelling	
Reading for big ideas *Nonfiction readers look for ways information fits together into bigger ideas.*	At points during the reading, pause and consider: • How does the information seem to go together? • What big idea(s) is this author trying to make a point about?	
Determining author's purpose and point of view *Nonfiction readers are aware of author's reason for writing and bias, and use this as they judge the validity of the information.*	• Consider the inclusion or exclusion of facts • Watch for a mix of fact and opinion • Pay attention to word choice and tone • Look for persuasive tools	
Making up our own minds *After reading many sources of information, nonfiction readers decide what they think about the issue/information.*	• Weigh everything that has been read against our own thinking • Decide what makes sense and feels right to us • Make sure there is evidence and/or facts to support our thinking	

Table 6–4

How do nonfiction readers make sure they really understand the cool information in the texts they're reading?			
Focus point	**How readers do this**	**What the talk might sound like**	**Being a text user and text analyst**
Reading with a wide-awake mind *Nonfiction readers pause in their reading, and say "Wow!"*	• Read in a way that allows you to notice: - Incredible facts - Numbers and/or information that seems amazing - What's happening in photographs and other features • Pause and let the information "sink in" • React to the information	*Wow. I didn't know penguins could be that big. It might be bigger than me.* *But look how tiny this one is. That's really tiny next to the big one!*	What does this text seem to really be about? What does this author seem to think? Why is the author presenting the information in this way? Is this author believable? What do I think?
Making sense of the information *Nonfiction readers don't just absorb information; they create understanding.*	• Compare and contrast new information to known information • Create analogies • Form visual images • Use what you already know • Reread or read on	*Jumps 6 feet . . . that's higher than me. It can jump over my head!*	
Asking questions and forming theories *Nonfiction readers question as they read and work actively to answer their questions.*	• Allow ourselves to wonder • Use what we already know about the topic and the world to form a theory • Draw from other sources of information • Read on and reread to confirm theory, or discard theory and form new theory	*Why is it jumping? I thought penguins couldn't do that.* *They're jumping to get out of the water. Hey—that's where their enemies are. I wonder if that's why they jump?*	

Table 6–5

Determining author's purpose and point of view is another fascinating study, especially when it comes to digging in to the art of persuasion. Children become very indignant when they realize that authors actually try to manipulate their feelings and decisions. Smart readers judge a text's validity based on these realizations. Readers must also consider how their own thinking aligns with the author's, and eventually make up their own minds. Once readers are aware of the various reasons authors write, and the ways authors try to persuade us, a study such as that in Table 6–6 will teach them to thoughtfully analyze text and make up their own minds, rather than believing everything they read. Again, the possible focus points are not all inclusive or necessarily linear.

	How do readers read and think critically?		
Focus point	**How readers do this**	**What the talk might sound like**	**Being a text user and text analyst**
Assessing the Facts *Nonfiction readers realize authors don't always tell us everything we need to know.*	We ask ourselves: • What do I know about this topic? • Did the author include all the facts, or is there a purposeful selection of facts? • Does the information seem to be all positive or all negative, or balanced? • Do the facts make sense to me?	*It makes it sound like everybody likes school uniforms. There's nothing about reasons why we shouldn't wear them. I'm not sure the author is telling us everything.*	
Differentiating Fact vs. Opinion *Nonfiction readers know authors might include a mix of fact and opinion, depending on their purpose.*	We pause and consider: • Can the information be proven, or is some of it opinion? • If some information is opinion, why is it here? What is the author doing?	*The author keeps saying they're great—I think it's just to persuade us. He can't prove that.*	Why does this author seem to think this way? Whose voice is not heard in this text? Does the world really work in this way? Should it? What do other authors and people think? What can I do to change or help things?
Assessing Word Choice *Nonfiction readers are alert for well-crafted texts that purposefully work to elicit a desired response.*	We are alert for: • Descriptive language • Strong adjectives or verbs • Phrasing that creates a purposeful mood or tone We consider the impact this language is having on us.	*Every time he talks about kids who aren't wearing uniforms, he makes them sound bad. If this was to inform or entertain, he wouldn't do that.*	
Determining author's purpose and point of view *Nonfiction readers are alert for the ways authors give away their own feelings on the topic or issue, and whether they are trying to sway the reader.*	We pause and consider: • What does this mix of fact and opinion tell me about the way this author is thinking, or her or his point of view? • What does the author's word choice tell me? • Is the author's point of view connected to her or his purpose?	*Because of the facts he chose to tell us, the facts that aren't included, and the word choice, It seems like he thinks uniforms are good. He's trying to convince us, too!*	
Noticing other persuasive tools *Nonfiction readers are alert for other ways authors attempt to control their thinking.*	Authors will use: • Quotes from experts • Photographs • Inclusive language (We all need to . . .)	*The picture shows kids in uniforms studying. He wants parents to believe uniforms make us smarter.*	
Making our own decision *Nonfiction readers make up their own minds.*	We ask ourselves: • Do I need more information? • Who can I read that has a different point of view? • What exactly do I think about this?	*A uniform won't change the way I act or think. He's wrong. I don't think uniforms will change anything, because . . .*	

Table 6–6

You may choose to introduce focus points as the text you choose presents the opportunity to do so.

When we push back at a text and discern what the author is doing, we are able to make smarter decisions about the content of the text. In Chapter 3, we listened in to a snippet of talk from a group of fifth-graders reading "Let's Rage Against 'Roids." Let's listen to more talk from the end of that same lesson.

MARCO: If some kids don't think and take steroids, it's not a death wish. So they take it—they don't want to die, just have muscles like the picture.
MADELINE: Yeah, but he says death wish on purpose—even though it's not true.
ANDRE: But he wants to persuade! But he's still, like, right about not taking them. I'm not taking them, 'cuz of all the other stuff. *Heart attack, stroke . . .*
PATTY: That's why he said all that. It's facts that stick with his point of view.

These readers argued over the crafting of the content, determined author purpose, and judged the message to still be valid. We should all be so discerning with everything we read!

Drawing from Many Sources: Reading, Thinking, and Talking Between Genres

TROY: Hey, this one doesn't talk about the venom.
MANNY: Venom?
TROY: Yea, the venom when he bites. Remember, from yesterday, it runs down his teeth and goes into the prey?
MANNY: Oh, yeah—that made the Gila monster sound scary.
VANESSA: This isn't scary. Maybe there's two kinds of Gila monsters!

This brief conversation was a spontaneous outburst from my second- and third-graders two days into their first instructional experience on reading, thinking, and talking between texts. The day before, we had read an excerpt on Gila monsters from *This Place Is Dry*, a factual nonfiction text about deserts, by Vikki Cobb (1993). We discussed the text through the lens of author's purpose, author's point of view, factual information, the crafting of the information, and its relationship to author's purpose and author's point of view.

In the children's thinking, Cobb seemed to have written an informational piece, which presented the Gila monster as a creature to be avoided. The warnings about the bite of the Gila monster, and the way it hangs on after the bite— *This gives the venom a chance to run down the grooves of their teeth into the wound.*—seem carefully crafted to get this point across and enhance the author's point of view: Gila monsters are dangerous!

When the above conversation erupted, we had just finished a first read of "Shy Monster," from Frank Asch's *Cactus Poems* (1998). Our focus this day was to uncover Asch's purpose (to persuade as well as inform). Asch presented the Gila monster as a shy, misunderstood creature—*I'm called a monster, I don't know why*—personified with the "I" voice to manipulate the reader into believing Gila monsters aren't the true monster Cobb presents. I was pleased to hear the children picking up on this difference even before we had dug into "Shy Monster."

Our next day's work would be thinking and talking between the two texts. We needed to consider what factual information we had learned from Cobb's informational piece, and whether Asch had included or excluded the same information. If included, did both authors craft the information with the same tone and intensity? Why or why not? How does this relate to author's purpose and point of view? Did one author choose to leave out information? Again, how does this relate to purpose and point of view? Are either of the texts a reliable source of information? Are other sources needed? Are there really two kinds of Gila monsters, or does author purpose and point of view motivate the authors to present the same creature in different ways?

Learning to read and think between sources of information is an essential skill in today's world. Children must learn to gather credible information from many sources, synthesize what they read, form an opinion, and articulate their own thoughts. When readers take on multiple texts around a theme or topic, their own thinking and conversation grow stronger. These multiple texts, or "text sets," may be true to one genre or a mixture of genre (e.g., nonfiction, realistic fiction, historical fiction, nonfiction poetry) gathered around a topic, theme, or big idea. When children are new to reading, thinking, and talking between texts, we begin with text sets created around a topic, as a topic's concreteness is more supportive than theme or big ideas.

The chart in Table 6–7 contains some possible focus points for reading, thinking, and talking between texts. Again, it is not intended to represent the entirety of the work.

The third-grade teachers at Webster Elementary designed a series of lessons as the first experience in a study of reading, thinking, and talking between texts. They selected wolves as a topic, as many of the children seemed to gravitate toward wolf books when selecting text. The experience began with a Read Aloud of *Wolves* by Gail Gibbons, an author the children knew and trusted as a source of factual information.

How do readers read, think, and talk between texts?			
Focus point	**How readers do this**	**What the talk might sound like**	**Being a text user and text analyst**
Constructing an understanding of each text *Readers need a deep understanding of each text on its own.*	• Make sense of facts • Determine big idea or theme • Determine author's purpose and point of view • Consider the mix of facts and opinion	*This author thinks Gila monsters are mean. Listen to how he describes the bite.*	What do authors seem to think about this? Whose opinion is represented? Whose voice is left out? Does anyone benefit from this point of view? Is it fair to think in this way? What do I think is true? What should happen because of this? What is my role?
Comparing and contrasting *Readers need to read, think, and talk between texts to begin to build a body of knowledge.*	• Compare the above in two texts • Sort through the similarities and differences and use them to form understandings that make sense to you	*Some of the facts are the same, but this author tells more. And, he says they're shy. They only bite when they have to. They have different points of view.*	
Drawing in other sources *Readers gather as much information as possible to push their thinking*	• Draw in other texts • Continue to compare and contrast between all texts • Use the information in each to help understand the others	*What I'm finding now is that most authors are amazed by these creatures. But some, who worry about people's safety, make them sound scary.*	
Building toward a stronger understanding *Readers use their understandings of the facts and other's points of view to form their own opinion.*	• Sort through the information using what you've determined about each author's purpose and point of view • Form your own beliefs • Check your beliefs against the evidence and facts	*So, people don't agree. I wonder why not? The article said medicine was being made from them. We need to protect them. I think…*	

Table 6–7

Next was a Shared Reading of *The Wolf Packs Are Back,* a text from the third-grade collection of *Write Time for Kids* (Teacher Created Materials, 2000). From this text, children came to realize that, although they all loved wolves, other people had differing views on wolves. Although the text presented the differing views, Jesse Harrison's children detected a pro-wolf persuasive stance on the part of the author. As they compared and contrasted this text with *Wolves,* the children began to tease out a pro-wolf point of view from Gail Gibbons that had not been noticed previously.

After this was a Shared Reading of "Howl" from *Cactus Poems*, by Frank Asch. Jesse's children recognized the persuasive stance immediately in this piece. By the end of the experience, the children were weaving this text into their understandings from the other two texts.

KIARRA: He (Frank Asch) used the wolf's voice 'cuz he knew we would feel sorry for it. That's even more persuading than the wolf piece we read yesterday.
JERRELL: Yeah, he talks about the sheep, but makes it like the wolves have to kill them. It didn't have blood to make the wolves seem nicer.
RAMIKA: I think they all like wolves and want us to like them, too.
KEYSHA: Well, not just that, but stick up for them, too.

Just to shake things up, I decided to bring an editorial from a Montana newspaper sharing a rancher's account of a wolf attack on his sheep into the mix in Marika Nieratko's classroom. This piece portrays the opposite point of view from what the children had been reading. This snippet of talk came as we visited the piece a second time.

JORGE: He wants to kill them—the wolves. He's persuading—well, no, maybe just telling.
LORENA: No, no—it's persuading, 'cuz he tells how scared the sheep were.
KIELLAN: But, it's different from the others (pieces of text) because they have trouble with the wolves. If we just read this, we would think wolves are bad.
D'ANDREA: No, it's kind of like some of the people in that other—*The Wolf Packs Are Back*.
TIMOTHY: Yeah, this one's not just making us think wolves are good. Like Gail Gibbons and the others. How can we know?

The children were drawing on all the texts they had read with an awareness that authors purposefully craft texts to have an effect on us. As they talked, they were pushing back, questioning, and feeling slight frustration because of the differences in point of view.

Notice that in no way did we step in, interject our own point of view, or attempt to alleviate the frustration by "teaching" children the correct way to think about wolves. Rather, our job is to provide the medium that allows children to discover the issue itself, the sides of the issue, opportunity to consider both, and teach them to think and talk to construct and negotiate meaning. In this case, the slight frustration that the children felt fueled continued reading, and as they learned more, the children began to form their own thinking. These are ways of reading that begin to build habits of mind.

 ## First Steps Toward the Ultimate Goal: Drawing on All Studies to Think About Our World

It's late spring, and the children in Jeralyn's class have read, thought, and talked under the influence of many studies. They've become passionate readers who understand their role in the construction of meaning, and the importance of purposeful talk as a part of the process. Let's listen in on a conversation among three readers.

On this particular day, Anya, Isabelle, and Mercedes were clustered around one side of a round table, thinking and talking between a variety of texts about bats they had been reading. Included in the collection were articles, informational trade books, narrative nonfiction, and a fiction text. Predictably, the girls' conversation started with facts. As their thinking and talk progressed, however, they began pulling out big ideas, questioning author's purpose, and eventually questioning the ways of our world.

ANYA: I think he's (one author) saying we shouldn't be scared of bats. They help us.

ISABELLE: 'Cuz they eat insects. And I think he's persuading us to help, to think they're harmless.

MERCEDES: His point of view is don't be afraid. So is all of these authors.

ANYA: They—all the authors—they want to persuade us not to believe it.

ISABELLE: Yeah, 'cuz they all tell good facts about bats. Nothing bad.

ANYA: Even Stellaluna. It's not real, but the author makes Stellaluna so we care about her.

ISABELLE: And we'll protect them and stuff. People should do that—be fair to them.

MERCEDES: But this one—it shows in movies and some stories, like here . . . wait . . . here (flips through a magazine) . . . they (bats) seem like the bad guys. But it's the movies that make us think like that. They make us believe stuff like vampires. It isn't real, but people get scared of bats.

ANYA: Movies shouldn't do that because people believe them.

MERCEDES: They're not scary—not like what the movies makes people think. We should tell them (people) don't believe the movies when they try to make us think things. Movies always do that, and we shouldn't let them.

What's most striking in this conversation is the evidence of active, engaged reading. These are not readers who passively skim over facts or absorb them without questioning and pushing back. Their stance as readers is, "What are these authors saying and why, and how do I feel about this?" And, more importantly, these third-graders are beginning to envision acting on their understanding to create a more just world. When these girls transition to independent reading, I doubt they will revert to passivity. Engaging in studies of increasingly complex ways of thinking and talking about text has developed habits of mind.

Building Toward Independence

Moving Reading, Thinking, and Talking Down the Release of Responsibility Slide

By giving our students practice in talking with others,
we give them frames for thinking on their own.
—Lev Vygotsky

"I 'm reading slow because of all the talking in my head!" These joyous words, matter-of-factly tossed out by Troy during a reading conference, are a celebration of efforts to not only develop self-sufficiency with thinking and talking purposefully about reading, but also to create habits of mind for engaged independent reading. Although the talk in Troy's head still has ample room for gains in complexity, what puts this second-grader so far ahead is that he has already developed the understanding that reading is an active process. Troy knows that readers have conversations in their heads, even when they read alone!

Troy's success is the result of immersion in numerous and expanded opportunities designed to guide and support children toward an overarching goal of thinking, engaging in purposeful talk, and constructing and negotiating meaning for the purpose of developing "frames for thinking on their own." This chapter will explore a variety of instructional approaches, supports, and development of reflective abilities that compose the "with" opportunities on the Release of Responsibility Model. The drawing on page 53 (Figure 5–1) illustrates the amount of support from teachers and peers offered by each.

 ## Shared Reading

Shared Reading is a slightly less supportive instructional approach than Read Aloud, just a step down on the Release of Responsibility slide. It is most often thought of as a means of supporting emergent and early readers in their roles as text decoders and text participants. However, Sue Brown, author of *Shared Reading for Grade Three and Beyond*, emphasizes that, "One of the most important reasons for using Shared Reading beyond the first few years of school is to improve the quality and depth of students' thinking through discussions about texts" (2004, 75). When used in whole group or small group instructional situations, Shared Reading supports children of all ages in thinking and talking as text users, text participants, and text analysts.

Purposeful talk is a key feature of Shared Reading. During Shared Reading, we ask children to visually refer back to the written text as a means of sustaining thinking and conversation that builds purposefully toward rich meaning. Offering feedback to children during Shared Reading strengthens their decision-making and strategy use, and gives them the confidence to think and talk about challenging text in increasingly independent situations. Sue Brown reminds us that the purpose of feedback is not correcting children's ideas, but supporting them in their ability to reflect on their use of strategies.

The following snippet of conversation is from a Shared Reading lesson with my second- and third-graders. The text, "Amber Was Brave, Essie Was Smart," is the first poem in Vera B. Williams' collection by the same title. A section of the poem had been read, and, after listening in to the turn-and-talk conversations, I purposefully asked Desiree and Anthony to start the whole class conversation.

DESIREE: We talked about the stuff Essie does, because she does the cooking and the sandwiches and stuff.
ANTHONY: Yeah, we talked about it because that's what Moms do, and we said, 'Why is Essie doing that?' We had to figure it out. We think maybe Mom's too busy, and Essie, she's the kind of kid who doesn't want her mom to be stressed.
DESIREE: Yeah, because she (Mom) probably works and she's tired.

Once the children discussed Essie and her relationship with Mom, my feedback included explicit highlighting of their decision to discuss an important character and form a theory about her motivation to gain a deeper understanding, and the strategies used for this purpose. We held on to this thinking as we read on, stopping for turn-and-talks that allowed all to take on this same strategy and discuss Essie and her mom, as well as other crucial aspects of the text.

Despite strong instructional design and talk in the Read Aloud, without this slightly less supportive venue for practicing thinking and talking about reading in purposeful ways with feedback, many children are apt to revert back to retells, literal thinking, and unfocused talk when they head off to partner and independent reading.

 ## Guided Reading

Guided Reading is a small group instructional approach that lies one step further down the Release of Responsibility slide from Shared Reading. Guided Reading offers an opportunity to purposefully group children with similar needs for coaching in carefully selected texts. The lessons are a concentrated opportunity for children to interact with a text, relying on the teacher only to set the focus for reading, nudge them to take it on, and coach when necessary. The lesson design includes opportunities to talk prior to, during, and after reading.

Guided Reading supports children in taking on a primary instructional focus based on assessed needs, including the thinking that supports purposeful talk. It's also an ideal venue for coaching that talk. Talk behaviors such as listening with intent or pursuing a line of thinking to enable the construction of bigger ideas can be built into the stop-and-talk opportunities. This supports the primary focus, which always builds toward meaning-making, and improves the children's ability to engage in purposeful talk at the same time.

The size of a Guided Reading group (generally no more than six) may also provide a more comfortable, nurturing environment for shy or quiet children who are reluctant to speak in whole class situations. In addition to meeting with a Guided Reading group based on instructional need, children may be placed in additional groups when the level of reading is appropriate for the purpose of coaching their ability to talk about their thinking.

This coaching may include support with conversational behavior, listening with intent, or support in getting their idea out, with feedback on the result. As with Shared Reading, this feedback is crucial, as it allows children to feel the power of their intellectual effort, which in turns builds the confidence they need to participate on their own.

 ## Developing Reading Partnerships

It was Reading Workshop, and I was watching Sergio and Manny, two of my third-graders, from across the room. They were on the carpet, with Eve Bunting's *A Picnic in October* between them. This realistic fiction tells of an immigrant grandmother's yearly visit to honor the Statue of Liberty, and her grandson's struggle to understand why. The boys were excitedly flipping the pages, pointing, reading, and talking—seemingly all at once. I headed across the room, quite sure there was something going on worth listening to. As I sat down beside them, Manny was in the process of defending his thoughts on the main character in the story.

MANNY: No, no, you see, he was rude, but he changed.
SERGIO: Rude people don't change. He was making fun of everyone; he pretended to throw up . . .
MANNY: *That's* sick!
SERGIO: Yeah, but it was because he didn't want to go, he was like mad that they made him . . . and embarrassed too, like me when my mom makes me go . . .
MANNY: Yeah, at first, but look here at the end, see (flips the pages)—they're leaving, . . . here it is . . . see, he looks, he looks at the other family—it's like he gets it!
SERGIO: Let me see again (grabs book, studies the pictures on the pages Manny showed him, and whisper-reads the words on the page). Oh—you mean like now he gets why the Grandma thinks the statue is a big deal?
MANNY: Yeah, now he gets it.
SERGIO: So now it's in his heart, too?
MANNY: No—well OK, yeah, I guess it could be in his heart, but now he really gets that it's in his grandma's heart.

Sergio and Manny were engaged in an effort to truly understand their characters' feelings, the ways characters interact in texts, and changes in characters as stories unfold. Manny was the first to sense a change in the character. Through negotiation, Sergio was able to understand what Manny was saying, and they were then able to push their comprehension a little deeper.

Sergio and Manny's ability to read, think, and talk about their thinking without teacher orchestration is possible because of the support they offer each other as Reading Partners.

The work of Reading Partnerships has roots in the thoughtful planning of Read Alouds, Shared Reading, and Guided Reading. Even with strong instruction from these approaches, that last nudge down the Release of Responsibility slide as children take these ways of thinking and talking to independence is still too steep for some. Reading Partnerships gentle the slope. They are not an end, but a means of supporting students in taking those last steps toward independence.

Reading Partnerships are pairs of (or, at times, groups of three) children who support each other in reading, thinking, and talking about a text. They are thoughtfully formed with consideration for a mix of factors including reading level, reading preferences, and personality. Preferably, partnerships are long-term relationships that enable children to get to know each other as readers and build a history of shared text and conversations.

Developing strong partnerships to support the construction of meaning begins as early as kindergarten. I was visiting in Susie Althof's kindergarten classroom at Webster midyear, on what happened to be Tatina's first day in the class. Through daily minilessons, modeling, practice, and the co-creation of charts, Susie had long ago created purposeful partnerships. But this was something very new for Tatina. I pulled up next to Tatina and Shalisa, her new partner, as they settled down with an emergent text to read and discuss. Let's listen in.

SHALISA: Who goes first?
TATINA: Just read the book!
SHALISA: We have to take turns.
TATINA: How do we do that?
SHALISA: I go first, then you.
TATINA: I never did that.
SHALISA: I'll read the title.
TATINA: I've been here a while. I'm going home now.

Shalisa, who knows how partnerships work, was trying to coach and support Tatina. Tatina, on the other hand, was unsure of the partnership process and reading and talking with this much independence. It all seemed overwhelming to her—so much so, that she decided she just might go home!

However, just three weeks later, I was able to listen to Tatina and Shalisa work as partners again. The two girls were leaning in over a book, heads together, taking turns reading each page and supporting each other when necessary. After the read, the girls looked at each other.

SHALISA: Now we have ta talk.
TATINA: I like the favorite part . . .

SHALISA: Don't do the last part. That's my favorite part.
TATINA: OK, I'll talk about this favorite part . . .

While Shalisa is still taking the lead, Tatina now understands how partnerships work, and enjoys the social aspect of the learning, decoding support, and co-construction of meaning provided by the partnership.

When children first begin to explore Reading Partnerships, teaching a uniform "read one page out loud together (or taking turns), stop, think, and talk" process offers support. It is an easy habit for children to fall in to, and allows them to put their energy into thinking about the text as they read and build purposeful talk.

But reading an entire book together and stopping every page to talk is not the most natural way to read. As readers, we may progress through several pages before our thinking builds to a point where we need conversation, or we may have huge "ah-ha!" or "hold-on!" moments midpage that need immediate conversation. And, while primary students and/or emergent and early readers may be delighted with and supported by reading the text out loud to each other, at some point in the process of becoming a proficient reader, children's preference shifts toward silent reading, with the freedom to speed up, slow down, and/or reread as necessary.

So, as partner talk strengthens, we create a flexible process for engaging in a flow between Independent Reading and Partner Reading. The first step is for partners to plan for a mix of Independent Reading and partner talk. There is no absolute, "everyone in the class needs to do it this way" formula for this. Differentiation based on children's ability to stay thoughtfully engaged with text is a must. Some children who struggle to read with engaged, active minds, or our aerobic learners who struggle just to settle down with a book, may need to stay immersed in their reading partnership, perhaps continuing with the "read a page and talk" process for the entire reading time.

Other children will be ready to use their partnership as a scaffold for an increasing amount of Independent Reading time. These children may begin with a quick partner meeting before heading off to read. This quick meeting supports the readers in getting the text and their previous conversation back in their heads if continuing with a text, or gaining a sense of the read if they had selected a new text, and planning for their reading. As partners move into Independent Reading, most sit next to each other in case they come to a "need to talk now!" place in the text.

As children read and think about their reading on their own, they plan for a second partner meeting before the workshop wraps up. This planning includes active, engaged thinking while reading, and taking action on those thoughts in a way that allows the reader to hold on to their thinking for the upcoming conversation. This action may include jotting on sticky notes and attaching them to the appropriate pages of their book for quick reference back to the text, or jotting notes in a reading log.

Preparing for a partner conversation during independent reading causes children to anticipate the content of the upcoming conversation and to consider not only their ideas, but how to support their thinking, and possible alternate points of view. Reading in this way helps to set the habits of mind that children will need as members of a literate community, and to push their thinking when reading on their own.

 ## Conferring into Reading Partnerships and Independent Reading

Conferring into Reading Partnerships or Independent Reading allows us to check on the development of habits of mind and the level of comprehension readers are constructing. Carl Anderson, author of *How's It Going?* (2000), reminds us that conferences are conversations. Engaging in real conversation provides us the best window into children's thinking. While conferences do offer us the opportunity to ask questions as we talk, it's not a rapid fire of predetermined questions. The questions flow from a theory of the reader that we form as we converse with her or him.

When children are reading, thinking, and talking in partnerships, we are able to check in on and assess both readers' meaning-making process and their ability to talk purposefully about their thinking. When conferring into partnerships, we are able to assess a child's ability to listen with intent, pursue a line of thinking, and negotiate meaning. We teach and coach strategic abilities, and we also teach and coach purposeful talk, reminding them of the conversational behavior they need to be using and aspects of meaning-making that are strengthened through talk.

During conferring, the work of a reader or partnership may be highlighted for others using a "fishbowl." Just as the inquisitive gather around a fishbowl to observe and admire the beauty and behavior of its contents, we briefly gather readers around their peers to watch, listen, and learn from their process. For instance, as Manny and Sergio discussed the characters in *A Picnic in October*, other readers may have been cued to gather to observe the two boys' conversational behavior, consider the content of their talk, and study the strategies used to think and talk in this way, and the result. During a fishbowl, I support the spectators in focusing on the aspects of the thinking and talking that merit their attention, discuss the way the thinking and talking supported meaning-making, and encourage all readers to return to their own reading, thinking, and talking with this same behavior as a goal.

 ## Moving into Literature Circles

Literature Circles, as Harvey Daniels and Marilyn Bizar describe them in *Teaching the Best Practice Way* (2005, 2), are "peer-led circles patterned after adult reading groups." Literature Circles are an ideal opportunity for children to read with the support of peers in a productively social situation.

Literature Circles, like partnerships, help children to develop the habits of mind that will support their independent efforts. Of the two, Literature Circles may be slightly more challenging, as conversing in a group with more members but no teacher orchestration requires a greater degree of conversational skill than does talking in partnerships. With more members, it's easier for individuals in the group to be less accountable, or even silent. Quiet children may fade into the background. Also, with more ideas and/or points of view, it is easier for the talk to become disconnected or unfocused.

As a support, children will need minilessons to teach thinking and talking in a larger group with less teacher support. The children need to learn strategies for holding themselves and others accountable, inviting and expecting quiet members to contribute, and monitoring the purposefulness of their talk and the negotiation of meaning.

Picture books or short text are a wonderful support as children begin Literature Circles. Well-chosen picture books are complex enough to require conversation to negotiate and construct stronger meaning, but are short enough that children are better able to hold on to details and locate parts of the text while talking. The shorter length also offers the opportunity to practice the process of planning for reading, meeting to talk, and managing purposeful conversation that constructs meaning in larger groups several times over, from start to finish, in just a few weeks.

As the children think and talk together, we are able to observe, confer, and mine their work for minilessons, strengthening the process day by day. This way, when the children take on their first lengthy read in Literature Circles, they have many successful experiences under their belts to draw from.

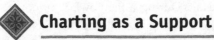

Charting as a Support

LISSETT: The author's point of view is . . . what? I can't find it!

DONNIE: Wait, let's see what the chart says. (Both look in the direction of a particular classroom chart.) Hey, that's it! We forgot to think about word choice. How does he say stuff?

LISSETT: Let's go back to this part, where he talked about . . .

In *Tools of the Mind* (1996), authors Elena Bodrova and Deborah J. Leong discuss Lev Vygotsky's explanation of mediators, or temporary scaffolds, which support the learner on the journey toward independence. Charts are one example of mediators in the learning environment that can be used to support children in increasing independence with thinking and talking about their reading until these ways become habits of mind. Luckily for Lissette and Donnie, their sixth-grade classroom was filled with these supports.

Bodrova and Leong point out that "mediators exist first in shared activity, and then are appropriated by the child" (69). Based on this, we design lessons that facilitate the co-creation of charts that support children in their efforts to read, think, and talk about their thinking in increasingly independent situations. The snippet of conversation between Donnie and Lissett is a perfect example of the way these charts spark ways of thinking. Charts may take many different forms. Let's take a look at four different forms, and ways to ensure that they are purposeful and supportive for children.

Shared Experience Charts

We often create charts by recording a whole class shared experience with a benchmark text that resulted in the construction of deep comprehension. These charts are created using excerpts from the text and the children's thinking and purposeful talk about the text, which can then be referred back to in new learning situations. "Remember how we thought and talked through this text?" we prompt as we refer to a chart and encourage the children to embark on the same work in a new text.

Referring back to these charts in this way, or using them for more complex instructional purposes beyond the original experience, keeps shared experience charts from becoming static, mere wallpaper with no instructional purpose. The chart of the text *Sea Turtles* (Gibbons 1998) that was co-created by Jesse Harrison and her third-graders (Figure 7–1), was later used side-by-side with a chart

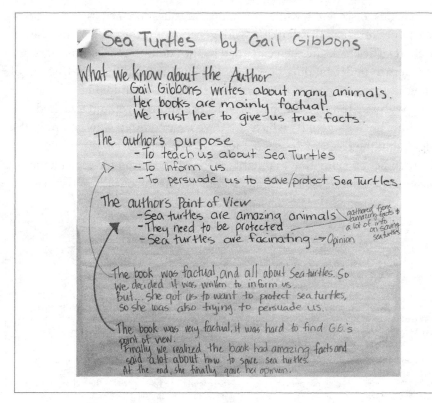

Figure 7–1 Sea Turtles chart

generated while reading *Into the Sea* (Guiberson 2000) to support children in thinking and talking between texts.

Some children are able to tease generalizations from the recorded shared experience charts to support their efforts to think and talk strategically with new texts. Other children need charts that expand upon the shared experience, explicitly outlining the strategies used to construct meaning within the benchmark text to support them in applying the strategies to their own reading. Strategy charts offer this added support.

Strategy Charts

Strategy charts are created as children explore big questions about reading, such as "How do readers get to know what's in a character's heart?" or "How do nonfiction authors try to persuade us?" These charts capture the process and strategies discovered while pursuing the question across many texts. Excerpts from texts and the thinking work generated by the children are part of these charts. The charts are then extended by the addition of columns that support readers in understanding how their thinking enabled the construction of meaning in that text, and most important, strategies for thinking and talking this way with any text. The finished product is a strategy column attached to a series of anchor experiences, which serve as a reminder of how to apply the strategies and the result of doing so. Table 7–1 is a strategy chart built during a third-grade fiction study that highlights the strategies used for understanding characters. The chart in Table 7–2 comes from a fifth-grade study of persuasion.

How do readers get to know what is in a character's heart?			
Excerpt from text	**Our thinking about this part of the text**	**How our thinking helped us to construct meaning**	**How can I think this way with any text I read? (strategies)**
When they can't see me, I point to a spilled-over trash can. "Oh look!" I whisper. "Look how beautiful." *The Peepers,* by Eve Bunting	The boys are making fun of the peepers.	The boys are being mean. We think they are too teenager-ish to really get it. We're understanding what the boys are really like.	Readers need to think about what their characters say, and why.
Your brother carried you all the way home . . . *My Rotten Redheaded Older Brother,* by Patricia Polacco	He really does care about Patricia.	They're just like typical brothers and sisters. They fight, but they really do love each other.	Readers need to think about the interactions between the characters.
And my father thought, *Boy, I'd like to see Nicky's face if I threw a tomato instead of the ball* . . . *The Summer My Father Was Ten,* by Pat Brisson.	He's only thinking about his own fun and not thinking about Mr. Bellavista.	The father is complex. We're understanding that he's a good person who can be impulsive sometimes.	Readers need to think about what characters think, and why.
You're such a person, Larnel! *Mrs. Katz and Tush,* by Patricia Polacco	That's meant in a nice way.	Mrs. Katz and Larnel are developing a special relationship.	Readers need to think about what other characters say or think about each other.

Table 7–1

How do nonfiction authors try to persuade us?			
Text excerpt	Our thinking about this part of the text	How our thinking helped us to construct meaning	How can I think this way with any text I read? (strategies)
Let's Rage Against 'Roids. "Let's Rage Against Roids." Write Time for Kids	Rage means get real mad. The author wants us to get mad.	If we get mad, we'll agree with the author.	Be aware of words that attempt to create strong emotions.
Let's Rage Against 'Roids. "Let's Rage Against Roids." Write Time for Kids	Let us—like we're going to do it, too.	The author wants us to feel like we're part of this.	Watch for inclusive language or an invitation from the author to join her or him.
Clear blue sea . . . beautiful underwater cities. *The Coral Reef Crisis* Exploring Nonfiction	This sounds wonderful.	The author did this on purpose to make us agree with him.	Be suspicious of descriptive language that purposefully creates a specific image.
The most exciting adventures of our time . . . "To the Moon, Mars and Beyond" by James R. Arnold, *The San Diego Union*, January 25, 2004.	He thinks going to Mars is the coolest thing.	His opinion makes us feel like it's cool, too.	Be aware of the author's insertion of opinion with facts.
Shy around people . . . humans aren't on their menu. "Swimming with Sharks," June 2002 issue of *Ranger Rick Magazine*.	It sounds like we're safe.	All the facts make us like sharks. We know people get killed by sharks, but the author doesn't tell about that.	Some authors only give us the facts that support their side of the issue.
"You should be much more afraid of bees and wasps," says Brandon Cole. "Swimming with Sharks," June 2002 issue of *Ranger Rick Magazine*.	He's saying we really shouldn't be afraid of sharks.	We're supposed to believe him because he knows a lot about sharks.	Authors quote "experts" or important people because they think we will believe what they say.

Table 7–2

Guiding Questions Chart

Questions that push children's thinking are another way of crafting charts that serve as external mediators. After specific questions are modeled and used to push thinking and talking in more supportive instructional situations, recording the questions reminds children to continue thinking in these ways as they construct meaning independently. Figure 7–2 is a chart of guiding questions used in a primary classroom to prompt and support thinking and talking about Folk Literature.

Procedural Charts

While the previous charts support children with the content of their talk, at times the children need the same level of support with conversational behavior. Charts that guide partners or small groups with talk behavior remind them that talk is a social as well as an intellectual endeavor.

A procedural chart for a kindergarten or first-grade classroom may remind children of behaviors such as the need to sit close together, look at each other, listen with intent, and ask questions. However, a procedural chart for an upper-grade classroom will be more in-depth, such as the chart from a sixth-grade

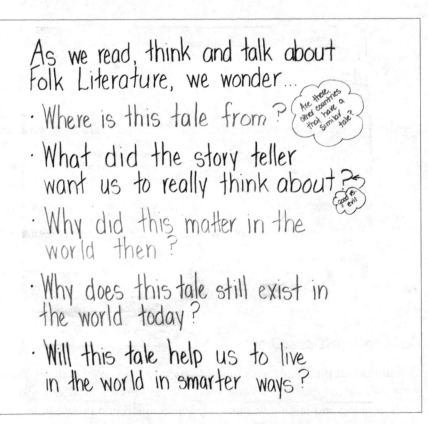

Figure 7–2 Folk literature chart

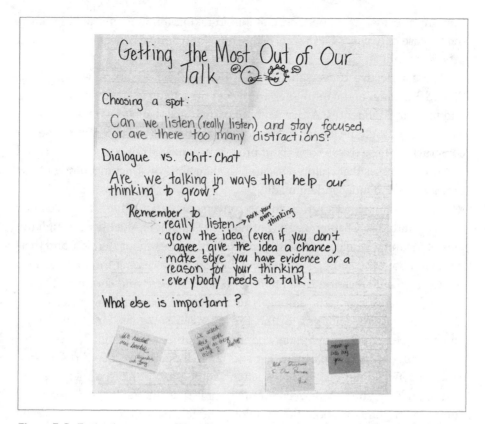

Figure 7–3 Getting the most our of our talk

classroom in Figure 7–3, which includes a reminder to pursue a line of thinking, and construct bigger ideas.

The "bones," or organization of charts can be formatted ahead of time, but the content of the chart must not be prescripted! To be meaningful, the children must recognize their own thinking on the chart, and understand the process that led to that thinking. Once the charts are created, minilessons that model the use of the chart and allow partners to try out thinking and talking in these ways with class and teacher support are essential.

The Role of Reflective Thinking

In Chapter 3, we discussed David Perkins' definition of reflective intelligence as a type of intelligence formed by developing the ability to reflect on one's own thinking process. As we support children in taking thinking and talking down the Release of Responsibility slide, taking time for reflective conversations around process is a must.

These reflective conversations begin during Read Aloud or whole group Shared Reading, and continue as we meet with children for Guided Reading and reading conferences. As we wrap up each lesson, we need to take the time to debrief through the lens of the meaning constructed, and the process used to construct it. These discussions about process become part of our charting, and it is these processes that children use to negotiate and construct meaning in their partnership and independent reading.

As an example, let's return to the conversation about "Let's Rage Against 'Roids," started in Chapter 3 and continued in Chapter 6. A debrief through the lens of meaning would wrap up the children's thinking about steroids, and their decision about the author's persuasive purpose. But a debrief through the lens of process would focus on their attention to the author's word choice and inclusion and exclusion of facts, among other persuasive tools, and how this attention to the author's crafting of the text changed some readers from strong agreement to agreement with only parts of the author's thinking.

As children read in partnerships and independently, we need to set aside time for reflection as well. This reflection can be part of their partner talk and part of the workshop share. What's important is that children have time for and support with thinking about their thinking and talking for the purpose of doing both in smarter ways, and creating habits of mind.

 ## The End Result

Over time, we should see and hear evidence of the cumulative effect of instructional experiences in reading, thinking, and talking and opportunities to practice with supports along the Release of Responsibility slide. Our children should be emerging from these experiences not only as stronger meaning-makers capable of orchestrating their own conversations and negotiating with others for the purpose of constructing meaning, but as critically aware thinkers who value the thinking of others.

The following conversation from a reading conference with Jailyn illustrates a child who is developing these habits. Jailyn was reading a Bruce McMillan book, *Nights of the Pufflings*, a touching nonfiction narrative about children in Iceland who pull together every year to help pufflings navigate their way to the sea on their first night flight. Without their help, many pufflings would become lost due to confusion created by city lights.

As I watched Jailyn, she was seemingly mesmerized by the text. She flipped pages back and forth, moving from photographs to text and back again, rereading, and jotting on sticky notes. After each pause, she quickly reengaged with her reading. There were several sticky notes protruding from pages already read. I began the conference with my usual, "What are you thinking?"

Jailyn began by discussing the way the children in the text helped the pufflings. Then, she said something that startled me. "I thought they [the children in the text] just do it to care for nature, but I know some kids [in our class] would say the people have to help," Jailyn explained, "because they shouldn't have lights and dogs where the pufflings have to fly. So now I think they are caring, but maybe they also they feel guilty 'cuz, it's their lights that, like, well, that make the pufflings get lost."

"How do you know that some of the kids would think that?" I asked.

"Well, it's like when we talked about *The Great Kapok Tree*," Jailyn said, pointing in the general direction of the Rain Forest tub in the nonfiction section of the library. "Some kids said the man shouldn't cut down the tree and live where the animals have to be. But people, they have to live places. But still, we thought they feel like, well, guilty."

"Wow, what made you think about all of this?"

"When I'm reading, and, well, always I wonder, what would everybody—all the kids—how do they think about this?"

Jailyn read with the posture of one who not only expects differing points of view, but values these differing views as a means of pushing her own thinking. She used previous conversations to anticipate what others would think, and was flexible enough to integrate that thinking with her own. Horace Mann once said, "Habit is a cable; we weave a thread of it each day, and at last we cannot break it." Through reading, thinking, and talking about her thinking with others, Jailyn is weaving a cable. She is forming the habits of mind that will enable her to construct meaning regardless of levels of support.

By teaching our children to read, think, and talk about their thinking, we enable them not only to have purposeful conversations that construct meaning with others, but also to have raging conversations in their own heads, even when thinking alone. In this way, we create self-sustaining, purposefully literate beings who question, build on the thinking of others, pursue more information, seek out and actually listen to other points of view, and in the end, make up their own minds.

Being literate by this definition is not an end, but a means of achieving a larger goal. We as individuals and collectively as a society invest in the effort to become literate to serve a grander purpose: the ability to take part in an intellectual exchange of ideas that constantly enlightens us, guides us, and helps us continually rethink our physical, social, political, and economic environment.

Through purposeful talk, we create constructivist thinkers who will be poised to become the innovators of the new economy, the newer economies yet to come, and more important, the guardians and continuous authors of a fair and just participatory democracy. They will live in a world that hasn't forgotten the value of dialogue.

Appendix
Core Text Choices for Fiction Study

The following are just a few titles from my very long list of favorite picture books, which may be used to create a set of core texts for a study of story elements, change, and theme. The books are divided into a list for primary children, and a list for upper grade children, but this designation is not absolute. The ultimate deciding factor for your text selection is your students.

Possible text choices for creating a core of books for primary children:

Harriet, You'll Drive Me Wild! by Mem Fox

> This is the hilarious story of a young girl who tries her mother's patience to the breaking point. It illustrates the power of the very special love between a mother and a child.

You and Me, Little Bear by Martin Waddell

> One in a series of tales about these wonderful bears, this story tells of the clash between the simple playfulness of Little Bear and the responsibilities Big Bear must shoulder. This joyful story tells of patience, love, and the need for a little fun in everyone's life.

Chrysanthemum by Kevin Henkes

> Chrysanthemum, a happy and confident child, goes to kindergarten and must find a way to deal with teasing. A funny but touching story, *Chrysanthemum* is about believing in one's self, the hurtfulness of teasing, and the power of a simple, kind gesture.

Julius, Baby of the World by Kevin Henkes

> Lilly, star of *Lilly's Purple Plastic Purse,* shows her disdain for her new little brother, Julius. But unkind words from a visiting cousin reveal Lilly's deepest, truest feelings. This is a funny but serious story of sibling rivalry, jealously, and the protective love of an older sister.

Thunder Cake by Patricia Polacco

> A frightened young Patricia must endure the ferocious thunderstorms at her Babushka's Michigan farm. Patricia learns that bravery comes from facing your fears, thanks to her wise and loving Babushka.

Memory String by Eve Bunting

> Laura clings sentimentally to a string of buttons, each representative of a special family memory, as she tries to deal with her new stepmother. Laura learns that we can make room in our hearts for someone new without letting go of those who mean so much to us.

Sunshine Home by Eve Bunting

> When Timmy and his family visit Gram in a nursing home, he realizes that all the adults are pretending to be happy rather than letting on to their real feelings. *Sunshine Home* is a passionate story about love, honesty, and hope.

Chicken Sunday by Patricia Polacco

> Patricia and her friends' hopes of earning money to buy a gift for Miss Eula Mae are dashed when they are wrongly accused of vandalism. Rather than despair, they work to earn the trust of the one person who can help them. This touching story tells of honesty, a strong work ethic, and love.

Possible text choices for creating a core of books for upper-grade children:

Your Move by Eve Bunting

> This story, told through the voice of ten-year-old James, is about the allure of gang life. James must choose between coolness and common sense, while his younger brother watches on. This story speaks to our need to belong, and how difficult it can be to do what is right.

Strong to the Hoop by John Coy

> James is unexpectedly faced with an opportunity to play a game of four-on-four with the older boys, and has an opportunity to prove himself in the process. This fast-paced story is about perseverance, the result of hard work, and the power of confidence.

The Other Side by Jacqueline Woodson

> Young girls challenge a physical and metaphorical fence as they develop a friendship more powerful than the cultural constraints of the time. This beautiful story displays the power of innocent curiosity, friendship, and acceptance.

An Angel for Solomon Singer by Cynthia Rylant

Solomon, who lives alone in a men's hotel in New York, longs for friendship and the comfort of home. A chance visit to the Westway Café and a waiter named Angel help him realize that friendship can make any place feel like home.

The Summer My Father was Ten by Pat Brisson

A young girl, planting a garden with her father, shares a story her father tells her every year, and in doing so imparts the importance of the garden. The reader is transported back to the father's childhood and follows the development of his unlikely friendship with Mr. Bellavista. This story dances around the true meaning of friendship, acceptance, and ways of honoring those who mean the most to us.

Freedom Summer by Deborah Wiles

This unsettling story, which takes place in Mississippi during the summer of 1964, tells of a small town's reaction to the Civil Rights Act. Told through the eyes of a young boy, this is a story about racism, friendship, and the triumph of the human spirit.

Gleam and Glow by Eve Bunting

Based on the real story of a Bosnian family, this book depicts the flight of Viktor and his family during the Bosnian civil war. Before they go, Viktor must release his new fish into the pond by the family home. Against all odds, the fish survives, as does the family and their home. This story tells of the power of hope, resiliency, and the gift of life.

The Harmonica by Tony Johnston

Based on the story of a Holocaust survivor, this gripping narrative tells of a young boy separated from his family in Poland and taken to a concentration camp. His only tie to his family is the harmonica his father gave him, which he hides to secretly play music by Schubert. This story examines the darker side of humans and the power of music to sustain us in the most difficult of times.

References

Abbott, John. 1997. "New Knowledge About the Biological Nature of Learning." In *Upside Down and Inside Out: A Challenge to Redesign Education Systems to Fit the Needs of a Learning Society.* New Horizons for Learning, www.newhorizons.org/trans/abbott2.htm.

Allington, Richard. 2002. "What I've Learned About Effective Reading Instruction." *Phi Delta Kappan* 83 (June): 740–747.

Allington, Richard, and Peter Johnston. 2002. *Reading to Learn: Lessons from Exemplary Fourth-Grade Classrooms.* New York: Guilford.

Anderson, Carl. 2000. *How's It Going?* Portsmouth, NH: Heinemann.

Beck, Isabel, Margaret G. McKeown, and Linda Kucan. 2002. *Bringing Words to Life: Robust Vocabulary Instruction.* New York: Guilford Press.

Beck, Isabel, Margaret G. McKeown, Rebecca L. Hamilton, and Linda Kucan 1997. *Questioning the Author.* Newark, NJ: International Reading Association.

Bodrova, Elena, and Deborah J. Leong. 1996. *Tools of the Mind.* Englewood Cliffs, NJ: Prentice Hall, Inc.

Bohm, David. 1996. *On Dialogue.* New York, NY: Routledge

Bomer, Randy, and Katherine Bomer. 2001. *For a Better World: Reading and Writing for Social Action.* Portsmouth, NH: Heinemann.

Brown, Sue. 2004. *Shared Reading for Grade Three and Beyond: Working It Out Together.* Wellington, New Zealand: Learning Media Limited.

Brunner, Jerome S. 1996. *Toward A Theory of Instruction.* Cambridge, MA: Harvard University Press.

Cambourne, Brian. 1988. *The Whole Story.* Aukland, New Zealand: Ashton Scholastic Limited.

Cazden, Courtney. 2001. *Classroom Discourse: The Language of Teaching and Learning.* Portsmouth, NH: Heinemann.

Cole, Ardith Davis. 2003. *Knee to Knee, Eye to Eye: Circling in on Comprehension.* Portsmouth, NH: Heinemann.

Daniels, Harvey, and Marilyn Bizar. 2005. *Teaching the Best Practice Way.* New York: Stenhouse.

Dewey, J. 1916. *Democracy and Education.* New York: Macmillan.

Dudley-Marling, Curt, and Dennis Searle. 1991. *When Students Have Time to Talk: Creating Contexts for Learning Language.* Portsmouth, NH: Heinemann.

Education Department of Western Australia. 1994. *First Steps Oral Language Developmental Continuum.* Portsmouth, NH: Heinemann.

Freebody, Peter, and Alan Luke. 1990. "Literacies' programmes: Debates and demands in cultural context." *Prospect: A Journal of Australian TESOL* 11:7–16.

Freire, Paulo. 2003. *Pedagogy of the Oppressed.* New York: The Continuum Publishing Group.

Hart, Betty, and Todd R. Risley. 1995. *Meaningful Differences in the Everyday Experiences of Young American Children.* Baltimore: Paul H. Brookes Publishing Co., Inc.

Isaacs, William. 1999. *Dialogue: The Art of Thinking Together.* New York: Random House.

Jensen, Eric. 1998. *Teaching with the Brain in Mind.* Alexandria, VA: Association for Supervision and Curriculum Development.

Johnston, Peter. 1997. *Knowing Literacy.* York, ME: Stenhouse.

———. 2004. *Choice Words: How Our Language Affects Children's Learning.* Portland, ME: Stenhouse.

Kohn, Alfie. 2000. *The Schools Our Children Deserve: Moving Beyond Traditional Classrooms and "Tougher Standards."* New York: Houghton Mifflin.

Marlowe, Bruce A. and Page, Marilyn L. 1998. *Creating and Sustaining the Constructivist Classroom.* Thousand Oaks, CA: Corwin Press.

New Standards Primary Literacy Committee. 1999. *Reading and Writing Grade by Grade.* Pittsburgh: National Center on Education and the Economy and the University of Pittsburgh.

New Standards Speaking and Listening Committee. 2001. *Speaking and Listening for Preschool Through Third Grade.* Pittsburgh: National Center on Education and the Economy and the University of Pittsburgh.

O'Keefe, Virginia. 1995. *Speaking to Think, Thinking to Speak.* Portsmouth, NH: Heinemann.

Opitz, Michael and Matthew D. Zbaracki. 2004. *Listen Hear! 25 Effective Listening Comprehension Strategies.* Portsmouth, New Hampshire: Heinemann.

Patterson, Kerry, Joseph Grenny, Ron McMillan, and Al Switzler. 2002. *Crucial Conversations: Tools for Talking When Stakes Are High.* Hightstown, NJ: McGraw-Hill.

Pearson, P. David, and Margaret C. Gallagher. 1983. "The Instruction of Reading Comprehension." *Contemporary Educational Psychology* 8:317–344.

Perkins, David. 1992. *Smart Schools.* New York: Simon & Schuster.

———. 1995. *Outsmarting I. Q.: The Emerging Science of Learnable Intelligence.* New York: Simon & Schuster.

———. 2003. *King Arthur's Round Table: How Collaborative Conversations Create Smart Organizations.* Hoboken, NJ: John Wiley & Sons.

Peterson, Ralph. 1992. *Life in a Crowded Place: Making a Learning Community.* Portsmouth, NH: Heinemann.

Resnick, Lauren. 1999. *Making America Smarter. Education Week Century Series* 18 (40): 38–40. www.edweek.org/ew/vol-18/40resnick.h18.

Senge, Peter. 1990. *The Fifth Discipline.* New York: Doubleday.

———. 2000. *Schools That Learn.* New York: Doubleday.

Stanfield, R. Brian. 2000. *The Art of Focused Conversation.* Gabriola Island, BC, Canada: New Society Publishers.

Vygotsky, L. S. 1978. *Mind in Society: The Development of Higher Psychological Processes.* Cambridge, MA: Harvard University Press.

Webber, Alan M. 1993. *What's So New About the New Economy? Harvard Business Review,* January–February, 4–11. .

Wheatley, Margaret J. 2002. *Turning to One Another: Simple Conversations to Restore Hope to the Future.* San Francisco: Berrett-Koehler Publishers.

Wink, Joan, and LeAnn Putney. 2002. *A Vision Of Vygotsky.* Boston: Pearson Education Co.

◈ Children's Books

Arnosky, Jim. 2002. *Watching Desert Wildlife.* Washington, DC: National Geographic Children's Books.

Asch, Frank. 1998. *Cactus Poems.* New York: Harcourt Brace & Co.

Bedard, Michael. 2002. *Emily.* New York: Dragonfly Books.

Brisson, Pat. 1999. *The Summer My Father Was Ten.* Honesdale, PA: Boyds Mills Press.

Bunting, Eve. 1998. *Gleam and Glow.* New York: Harcourt Children's Books.

———. 2000. *Memory String.* New York: Clarion.

———. 2001. *Peepers.* New York: Harcourt Children's Books.

———. 1999. *A Picnic in October.* New York: Harcourt Children's Books.

———. 2005. *Sunshine Home.* New York: Clarion.

———. 2000. *Train to Somewhere.* New York: Clarion.

———. 1998. *Your Move.* New York: Harcourt Children's Books.

Cameron, Ann. 1998. *The Stories Julian Tells.* New York: Yearling Press.

Cherry, Lynne. 2000. *The Great Kapok Tree: A Tale of the Amazon Rain Forest.* New York: Green Willow Press.

Cobb, Vikki. 1993. *This Place Is Dry: Arizona's Sonoran Desert.* New York: Walker Books for Young Readers.

Cooney, Barbara. 1999. *Eleanor.* New York: Puffin.

Coy, John. 1999. *Strong to the Hoop.* New York: Lee and Low Books.

Fox, Mem. 2000. *Harriet, You'll Drive Me Wild!* New York: Harcourt Children's Books.

Gibbons, Gail. 1998. *Sea Turtles.* New York: Holiday House.

———. 1995. *Wolves.* New York: Holiday House.

Goble, Paul. 1987. *Buffalo Woman.* New York: Aladdin Paperbacks.

Graves, Donald. 1996. *Baseball, Snakes, and Summer Squash: Poems About Growing Up.* Honesdale: PA: Boyds Mills Press.

Guiberson, Brenda Z. 2000. *Into the Sea.* New York: Henry Holt and Co.

Henkes, Kevin. 1988. *Chester's Way.* Hong Kong: Greenwillow Press.

———. 1996. *Chrysanthemum.* New York: Mulberry Paperback Books.

———. 1995. *Julius, the Baby of the World.* New York: Harper Trophy.

———. 2000. *Wemberley Worried*. New York: Greenwillow.

Hunter, Sara Hoagland. 1996. *The Unbreakable Code*. Flagstaff: Rising Moon.

Johnston, Tony. 2004. *The Harmonica*. Watertown, MA: Charlesbridge Publishing.

Keats, Ezra Jack. 1976. *The Snowy Day*. New York: Puffin.

London, Jonathan. 1998. *At the Edge of the Forest* Cambridge, MA: Candelwick Press.

McMillan, Bruce. 1995. *Nights of the Pufflings*. New York: Houghton Mifflin.

Penner, Lucille Recht. 2002. *Liberty! How the Revolutionary War Began*. New York: Random House.

Polacco, Patricia. 1992. *Chicken Sunday*. New York: Philomel.

———. 1994. *Mrs. Katz and Tush*. New York: Dragonfly Books.

———. 1998. *My Rotten Redheaded Older Brother*. New York: Aladdin.

———. 1990. *Thunder Cake*. New York: Philomel.

Ryan, Pam Muñoz. 1999. *Amelia and Eleanor Go for a Ride: Based on a True Story*. New York: Scholastic.

Rylant, Cynthia. 1996. *An Angel for Solomon Singer*. New York: Scholastic.

———. 1997. *Poppleton*. New York: Blue Sky.

Waddell, Martin. 1996. *You and Me, Little Bear*. New York: Scholastic.

White, E. B. 1974. *Charlotte's Web*. New York, NY: Harper Trophy.

Wiles, Deborah. 2001. *Freedom Summer*. New York: Atheneum.

Williams, Vera B. 2001. *Amber Was Brave, Essie Was Smart*. New York: Harper Children.

Woodson, Jacqueline. 2001. *The Other Side*. New York: Putnam Juvenile.

 ## Instructional Materials

Exploring Nonfiction. 2002. Huntington Beach, CA: Teacher Created Resources.

Let's Talk About It. 2004. New York, N.Y. Mondo Publishing.

Write Time for Kids. 2000. Huntington Beach, CA: Teacher Created Resources.

Index

Note: Pages with a *t* are tables; pages with an *f* are figures.